LOGO
LICIOUS!

**A TASTY COLLECTION OF THE BEST
LOGOS FROM AROUND THE GLOBE**

PELEG TOP

COLLINS DESIGN
An Imprint of HarperCollins Publishers

HarperCollins books may be purchased for educational, business, or sales promotional use. For information, please write: Special Markets Department, HarperCollins *Publishers*, 10 East 53rd Street, New York, NY 10022.

First published in 2010 by:
Collins Design
An Imprint of HarperCollins *Publishers*
10 East 53rd Street
New York, NY 10022
Tel: (212) 207-7000
Fax: (212) 207-7654
collinsdesign@harpercollins.com
www.harpercollins.com

Distributed throughout the world by:
HarperCollins *Publishers*
10 East 53rd Street
New York, NY 10022
Fax: (212) 207-7654

Art Direction: Peleg Top, Los Angeles, CA (pelegtop.com)
Design & Production: Shachar Lavi / Orange Bike Design, Los Angeles, CA (orangebikedesign.com)

Library of Congress Number: 2010926909

ISBN 978-0-06-197012-2

Produced by Crescent Hill Books, Louisville, KY
www.CrescentHillBooks.com

Printed in China

CONTENTS

Introduction 8

The Judges 10

Icons & Symbols 38

Wordmarks 106

Combinations 202

Index 332

"Good design is obvious.
Great design is transparent."

— Joe Sparano

ABOUT THE AUTHOR

Peleg Top is a master business coach and professional mentor to creative entrepreneurs. He helps creative business owners learn how to market and grow their businesses while leading well-balanced and spiritually fulfilling lives.

Peleg is a frequent speaker at national conferences, a regular contributor to leading design publications and blogs, and a creative community leader. He's also the co-author of *The Designer's Guide to Marketing and Pricing* (HOW Books).

Prior to his work as a business mentor, Peleg ran his own successful and profitable design agency for nearly two decades. Some of his notable clients include The Grammy Awards, Universal Music, Toyota, Quincy Jones, Steven Spielberg's Shoah Foundation, City of Hope, and the AIDS Healthcare Foundation.

Peleg is a designer at heart and an established curator of design excellence. This book is his fourth collection showcasing the best of design from around the world, which also includes *Design for Special Events* (Rockport), *Letterhead & Logo Design* (Rockport), and *Designing for the Greater Good: Best of Cause-Related and Nonprofit Design* (Harper Collins).

Outside his coaching and writing work, Peleg spends many hours in the kitchen cultivating his culinary skills and hosting fabulous dinner parties. He maintains work/life balance with regular yoga practice, meditation, and early morning nature hikes.

Visit www.pelegtop.com and say hello.

INTRODUCTION

This book contains more than just beautiful images. It's a compilation of hundreds of examples of high-level thinking. Each logo represents a careful thought process presented in a unique form of visual language. Each takes several different ideas and combines them together to create a new meaning in a smart, distinctive way. If you can look at a logo and say: "I get what they're trying to tell me," the designer has done his or her job well.

The primary purpose of this book is to provide a visual reference for brainstorming, both for designers and their clients. But logos are more than just branding and marketing tools. They're also cultural representations of the time they were created in.

Just as you can identify eras of fashion by glancing at a piece of vintage clothing, logos create and follow trends over time. Some companies update their logo every decade or so to stay current with the young or "hip" culture. Others strive for a timeless approach to remind you that a company is long-established or sticking to the roots of its founders. Collected together, the logos of any era provide insight into both the design industry and global culture as a whole. In the pages that follow, you'll find a snapshot of how the world is telling its stories today.

The logos in this book are grouped in three separate sections: icons (images that tell a complete story without words), type-driven wordmarks, and combination marks. We've chosen these groups mostly because they're useful for visual organization. Like many aspects of design, the logo style you choose is an intuitive, gut-level decision. There's no rhyme or reason to which type of logo a company should choose, and none of these three approaches is a clear winner when it comes to generating sales or brand recognition.

Nearly 1,000 logos are featured, selected from more than 4,000 entries by talented designers from around the world. The thirteen judges who were invited to participate are internationally recognized leaders in the design industry. Each has been practicing logo and brand identity development for over a decade. There's easily more than a century and a half of combined experience between them, but what's more important is that they've also distinguished themselves as influencers and trendsetters in the industry. The logos they design aren't just motivating buyers, they're affecting our culture and making change happen.

Every designer has a different perception of what a great logo is, so we've shared a little of each judge's philosophy to help you get a sense of their unique style and personality. When you look at their own work, showcased on pages 12–37, you'll definitely get a glimpse of the creative thinking behind the power of every great logo.

Peleg Top
Los Angeles

THE JUDGES

Jeff Barlow | Jelvetica

Darin Beaman | OIC

Joshua C. Chen | Chen Design Associates

Jonathan Cleveland | Cleveland Design

Jean-Marc Durviaux | DISTINC

Jeff Fisher | Jeff Fisher LogoMotives

Kit Hinrichs | Studio Hinrichs

Debbie Millman | Sterling Brands

Steve Morris | MORRIS

Robynne Raye | Modern Dog Design Co.

Cheryl Savala | Menagerie Creative

Rochelle Seltzer | Seltzer

Petrula Vrontikis | Vrontikis Design Office

" A great logo should have one (and only one) clear, intelligent, appropriate, memorable, unique, recognizable, legible, refined idea. And it should have a smart, well-run company behind it. Because no matter how brilliant the logo, it does not carry your value. It only REMINDS people of why you are valuable. "

Jelvetica
www.jelvetica.com

JEFF BARLOW

Jeff is the owner of the Seattle-based studio, Jelvetica. They specialize in helping their clients find the good ideas, then turn those ideas into strong brands.

His work and ideas have been featured in *Communication Arts*, the *HOW International Design Annual*, and the *HOW Self Promotion Annual*. His annual report and non-profit work have also been honored by *Creativity 27*, *Print* magazine, and other publications. His strategic and design experience includes work for Expedia, The National MS Society, Seattle International Film Festival, and WaMu. Aside from being a full-time principal and creative director at Jelvetica, he is also the President of AIGA Seattle, and a typography instructor at the School of Visual Concepts in Seattle, Washington.

Facing
THE Future

into the
woods

ROADKILL
PRODUCTIONS

BiLL NYE

hanker

" A good logo is…typically big and probably red. "

OIC
www.oicweb.com

DARIN BEAMAN

Darin Beaman was born in Pasadena, California, and received his MFA from Art Center College of Design Pasadena. He sold his first agency, Postmedia in 1998 and went on to co-found OIC an interactive and brand marketing agency where he serves as the Creative Director. The first logo Darin designed was for a hair salon—he received $200 and a haircut for his efforts. Since then he has produced work for Nestlé, NetApp, Sun Microsystems, Serena Software, Roxio, the Walt Disney Company, AMD, Intel and many other big impressive companies. Darin's work and blog can be found at oicweb.com.

> " A great logo needs to pique the viewer's curiosity and connect on an emotional level. "

Chen Design Associates
www. chendesign.com

JOSHUA C. CHEN

Joshua C. Chen is principal and creative director of Chen Design Associates, a creative communications agency in San Francisco, California. The firm has been recognized and featured internationally by leading design organizations and publications, including Communication Arts, Graphis, HOW, ReBrand, Print, STEP, Type Directors Club, AIGA, and Art Directors Club.

Joshua has over 18 years of professional experience in the fields of design, broadcasting, journalism, and music. His diverse background, as well as having lived in numerous countries, including Singapore, France, and Belgium, brings a global understanding of client objectives to each project.

Named one of 50 "people to watch" in 2003 by *GraphicDesignUSA*, Joshua is also author of three award-winning books, including *Fingerprint: The Art of Using Handmade Elements in Graphic Design* (HOW Books), and *Peace: 100 Ideas* (CDA Press), which was featured by A&E Television, dwell and Metropolis. A follow up to *Fingerprint* is in the works.

" A great logo is intriguing, simple, and timeless. **"**

Cleveland Design
www.clevelanddesign.com

JONATHAN CLEVELAND

As founder and principal of Cleveland Design, an award-winning graphic design and communications firm in Boston, Jonathan Cleveland is recognized both for his creative talent and his passionate belief in the power of great design. With more than 20 years' experience in marketing communications and graphic design, Jonathan brings to the table a strategic perspective and a solid business sense, together with a talent for creative solutions. His belief that great design springs from smart strategic planning has made him a trusted advisor to many global corporations— including Thomson Reuters, Fidelity Investments, and Sensitech— as well as numerous start-ups and non-profits. His work has been recognized through international design awards and under his leadership, Cleveland Design has been consistently named to the Top 25 Design Firms in New England by the *Boston Business Journal*. Jonathan is co-author of the book *Designing for the Greater Good* (Collins Design) with Peleg Top.

EMMANUEL
EPISCOPAL CHURCH

youngmariners

AMERICA'S CLASSIC 12 metre
SAILING FOUNDATION

POTTED UP™
creating city gardens

A great logo is a great logo. You recognize one when you see one, when you can remember one, and when you get that same gut feeling each time you see it… 〟

DISTINC
www.distinc.net

JEAN-MARC DURVIAUX

Jean-Marc Durviaux has been a specialist in visual communication for 20 years. Belgian-born, he studied in Brussels where he began his career at LHHS and Euro-RSCG. His curiosity brought him to California where he founded DISTINC in 2000.

Jean-Marc has an idealistic approach to design and communication. He has a strong belief that design not only plays an integral part in today's business, but also an important role in our society. He is convinced that good design can change behavior. Jean-Marc has helped numerous cause-based organizations position their brands, spell out communication strategies, and articulate visual language to successfully raise awareness about our responsibilities as good citizens.

Jean-Marc's work has been honored nationally and internationally by the American Institute of Graphic Arts, the Type Directors Club of New York, *Print* magazine, Rockport publishing, the British Photography Academy, and by the Creative Club of Belgium for art direction, graphic design, typographic excellence, and for environmental leadership in the practice of design.

" A great logo identifies, informs, inspires — and invites the viewer to learn more about a business, organization, product, or event. "

JEFF FISHER

Jeff Fisher LogoMotives
www.jfisherlogomotives.com

Jeff Fisher, author of *Logo Type: 200 Best Typographic Logos from Around the World Explained, Identity Crisis!: 50 redesigns that transformed stale identities into successful brands* and *The Savvy Designer's Guide to Success,* is the Engineer of Creative Identity for the Portland-based firm Jeff Fisher LogoMotives. A 32-year design veteran, he has been honored with over 600 regional, national, and international design awards and is featured in over 130 books about logos, the design business, and small business marketing.

Jeff serves on the HOW Magazine Board of Advisors and HOW Design Conference Advisory Council. The designer writes for *HOW* magazine, other industry publications, and many webzines and blogs. In addition, Jeff is a nationally recognized speaker, making numerous presentations each year to design organizations, design schools, universities, and business groups. He is often called upon to judge national and international design competitions.

2 BOYS IN A BED ON A COLD WINTER'S NIGHT

chameleon

HOLOCAUST REMEMBRANCE PROJECT Holland+Knight Charitable Foundation, Inc.

CAT ADOPTION TEAM

> "A great logo is not an illustration of what the company does or makes; it is a visual symbol of its spirit and personality. It should be unique and memorable; contemporary but not trendy; reproducible in multiple media and not color dependent. And it must be flexible enough to allow the company to grow and evolve and still feel relevant to who it is. "

KIT HINRICHS

Studio Hinrichs
www.studio-hinrichs.com

Kit Hinrichs studied at Art Center College of Design in Los Angeles, California. He served as principal in several design offices in New York and San Francisco before spending 23 years (1986–2009) as a partner of Pentagram, the international consultancy. In 2009, Kit opened an independent design firm in San Francisco called Studio Hinrichs. Kit's design experience incorporates a wide range of projects, including identity design, corporate communications, promotion, packaging, editorial and exhibition design.

Kit is a recipient of the prestigious AIGA medal in recognition of his exceptional achievements in the field of graphic design and visual communication, and his work is included in the permanent collections of the Museum of Modern Art, New York, the San Francisco Museum of Modern Art, and the Library of Congress. He is co-author of five books, including *Typewise, Long May She Wave,* and *The Pentagram Papers.*

@issue:

A great logo has the ability to define our beliefs, and signal our affiliations. For better or for worse, a great logo can make you feel better about who you are. 〞

DEBBIE MILLMAN

Sterling Brands
www.sterlingbrands.com

Debbie Millman has worked in the design business for over 25 years. She is President of the design division at Sterling Brands where she has worked on the redesign of global brands for Pepsi, Procter & Gamble, Campbell's, Colgate, Nestle, and Hasbro.

Debbie is President of the AIGA, the largest professional association for design. She is a contributing editor at *Print* magazine, a design writer at FastCompany.com and BrandNew.com, and Chair of the Masters in Branding Program at the School of Visual Arts in New York City. In 2005, she began hosting the first weekly radio talk show about design on the Internet. The show is called *Design Matters with Debbie Millman* and it is now featured on DesignObserver.com.

She is the author of *How To Think Like A Great Graphic Designer* (Allworth Press, 2007), *The Essential Principles of Graphic Design* (Rotovision, 2008) and *Look Both Ways: Illustrated Essays on the Intersection of Life and Design* (HOW Books, 2009).

A great logo is the visual distillment of the brand expression for an organization. If it's great, it creates a sensory experience that allows the viewer to instantly understand the organization being represented, while creating an emotional connection beyond mere understanding. 🙶

MORRIS
www.thinkmorris.com

STEVE MORRIS

For the past 16 years, Steven Morris has led MORRIS to become the leading young adult influence firm in the U.S. His firm creates cross-media strategy and design for brands including Sony Electronics, San Diego Chargers, San Diego Padres, ESPN, Northwestern University, and Mattel. They communicate with young consumer audiences across all media touch-points, including print, advertising, packaging, retail, promotions, motion, web, and interactive.

Born and educated on the East Coast, Steven holds an M.F.A. in Design from Temple University, Tyler School of Art. Steven's work in design has received hundreds of awards from national and international publications and competitions. *Business Week, STEP Inside Design,* and *HOW* magazines have looked to him as an advisor and editorial contributor on design, branding, and culture issues, and he has spoken at various national events. In addition to being an entrepreneur and creative director, Steven is a writer, educator, fine artist, and father.

" A great logo is simple. "

Modern Dog Design Co.
www.moderndog.com

ROBYNNE RAYE

Since co-founding Modern Dog Design Co. in 1987, Robynne Raye has continued to do work for entertainment and retail companies—both local and national—and counts poster, packaging, and identity projects as some of her favorite work. Recent clients include Coca-Cola, Adobe Systems Inc., Blue Q, Olive Green Dog Products, Shout! Factory, and Live Nation. Robynne has received recognition from every major design organization in the U.S. Her posters are represented in the permanent archives of the Louvre (Rohan Marsan wing), the Library of Congress, El Centro de Desarrollo des las Artes Visuales (in Havana, Cuba), Hong Kong Heritage Museum, Bibliotheque Nationale de France, Museum Fur Kunst und Gewerbe, the Warsaw National Museum, and the Cooper-Hewitt National Design Museum, among others. In March 2008, Chronicle Books published a 20-year retrospective focusing on Modern Dog's poster work. For more than 17 years, she has lectured and taught workshops, both nationally and internationally. Currently, she is an adjunct instructor at Cornish College of the Arts in Seattle, Washington.

A great logo personifies a brand, promises a message, and persuades an audience. 🙶

Menagerie Creative
www.menageriecreative.com

CHERYL SAVALA

With over 20 years of marketing and design expertise, Cheryl Savala leads the collective talent and energy at Menagerie Creative. She has directed creative for many of the industry's most successful entertainment campaigns, including *Star Wars, The Lord of the Rings, Planet of the Apes, Night at the Museum: Battle of the Smithsonian,* and the United Artists 90th Anniversary Celebration. Cheryl graduated from California State University Fullerton with a B.F.A. in Graphic Design and an M.F.A. in Illustration. Each semester, Cheryl returns to her alma mater to teach an upper division course focusing on entertainment design. Under her guidance, over 30 young talents have been recognized by *The Hollywood Reporter* Key Art Awards in the Annual Student Key Art Award Competition.

menagerie

A great logo is distinctive, memorable, and appropriate for the organization. It's built on a strong concept and graphically expresses the 'DNA' of the enterprise, to resonate and build connections with the intended markets.

ROCHELLE SELTZER

Seltzer
www.seltzerdesign.com

Rochelle founded Seltzer with a mission to build strategically focused, powerful design solutions for brand-savvy businesses and non-profits. She is passionate about the power of design for business—and for making our world a better place.

Seltzer's clients all have complex service, product, or technical information to share with discerning and sophisticated audiences. Seltzer develops distinctive and compelling solutions that resonate with those audiences. Rochelle oversees all projects and ensures the integrity and quality of the firm's work.

Rochelle earned a B.F.A. from Moore College of Art and Design. She is a member of AIGA and The Boston Club, and serves on non-profit boards. She speaks to business audiences on topics related to branding, marketing, and the power of design for business success. Rochelle was selected as a Top 10 Advertising and Marketing Professional by Women's Business Boston and is proud that the firm's work has been honored with numerous awards and recognition.

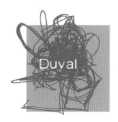

A great logo is a distinctive visual translation of the message a company or organization wants to convey. It is an essential tool for communication as it introduces and reinforces memorable associations between companies and customers.

Vrontikis Design Office
www.35k.com

PETRULA VRONTIKIS

Petrula Vrontikis has been a leading voice in graphic design and design education communities for over 20 years. Her work has appeared in over 100 books and publications, and is part of the permanent collection of the Library of Congress. She lectures at conferences, universities, and to professional organizations worldwide about her work with Vrontikis Design Office (35k.com), about graphic design education, and on the subject of inspiration. She has taught the senior graphic design studies course at Art Center College of Design in Pasadena since 1989. In 2007, Petrula received an AIGA Los Angeles Fellows Award honoring her as an essential voice raising the understanding of design within the industry and among the business and cultural communities of Los Angeles.

ICONS &
SYMBOLS

1

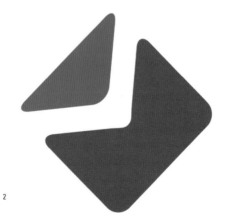

2

1

FB Productions
INDUSTRY: Music Productions
AGENCY: Blackspot Designs
LOCATION: Coral Springs, FL

2

MaxInvest Settlements
INDUSTRY: Settlements &
Retirement Fund Services
AGENCY: D&Dre Creative
LOCATION: Round Rock, TX

1

2

3

4

1
Luscious Garage
INDUSTRY: Auto Repair
AGENCY: Theory Associates
LOCATION: San Francisco, CA

2
Green Clean Moving
INDUSTRY: Local and Long
Distance Moving
AGENCY: Unexpected Ways
LOCATION: Marietta, GA

3
Paella Alfresco
INDUSTRY: Personal Chef
AGENCY: Roskelly Inc.
LOCATION: Portsmouth, RI

4
**The Tori Lynn
Androzzi Foundation**
INDUSTRY: Foundation
AGENCY: Roskelly Inc.
LOCATION: Portsmouth, RI

1

2

3

4

1

Plant Lovers Garden Gallery
INDUSTRY: Retail Nursery
and Landscape Design
AGENCY: Creative Madhouse
LOCATION: Fort Worth, TX

2

Shahal
INDUSTRY: Medical
AGENCY: Danny Goldberg
Design
LOCATION: Tel Aviv, Israel

3

Inner City Relief
INDUSTRY: Nonprofit
AGENCY: Bronson Ma Creative
LOCATION: San Antonio, TX

4

**Gobierno del Estado de
Michoacan, Mexico**
INDUSTRY: Social development
AGENCY: Caracol Consultores
LOCATION: Michoacán, Mexico

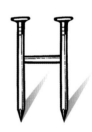

1
Uchenna
INDUSTRY: Bath & Body
AGENCY: Burn Creative
LOCATION: Carlisle, PA

2
Barkvarians
INDUSTRY: Pets
AGENCY: Bright Rain Creative
LOCATION: Maryland Heights,
MO

3
Upward Bound
Basketball Camp
INDUSTRY: Sports
AGENCY: Solak Design Co.
LOCATION: New Hartford, CT

4
Harding Construction
INDUSTRY: Construction
AGENCY: Scott Ott Creative
LOCATION: New Orleans, LA

1

2

1
University of California at Davis / Fire Dept.
INDUSTRY: Education
AGENCY: Gee + Chung Design
LOCATION: San Francisco, CA

2
University of California at Davis / Operations & Maintenance
INDUSTRY: Education
AGENCY: Gee + Chung Design
LOCATION: San Francisco, CA

1

2

3

4

1
University of California at Davis / Innovation & Quality Assurance
INDUSTRY: Education
AGENCY: Gee + Chung Design
LOCATION: San Francisco, CA

2
University of California at Davis / Architects & Engineers
INDUSTRY: Education
AGENCY: Gee + Chung Design
LOCATION: San Francisco, CA

3
University of California at Davis / Health & Safety
INDUSTRY: Education
AGENCY: Gee + Chung Design
LOCATION: San Francisco, CA

4
University of California at Davis / Facilities
INDUSTRY: Education
AGENCY: Gee + Chung Design
LOCATION: San Francisco, CA

1

2

3

1
**Washington Afterschool
Project**
INDUSTRY: Education
AGENCY: Weather Control
LOCATION: Seattle, WA

2
Westboro Nursery School
INDUSTRY: Education
AGENCY: idAPostle
LOCATION: Ottawa, Alberta,
Canada

3
**Wendy Weiner Interior
Design**
INDUSTRY: Interior Design
AGENCY: Orange Bike Design
LOCATION: Los Angeles, CA

1

2

3

4

1
Kleckner Consulting
INDUSTRY: Communications/PR
AGENCY: Bronson Ma Creative
LOCATION: San Antonio, TX

2
Bronson Ma Creative
INDUSTRY: Design
AGENCY: Bronson Ma Creative
LOCATION: San Antonio, TX

3
Gloria Alvaro
INDUSTRY: Business Coaching
AGENCY: Q
LOCATION: Wiesbaden,
Germany

4
One-to-One Solutions
INDUSTRY: Printing
AGENCY: Bronson Ma Creative
LOCATION: San Antonio, TX

1

2

3

4

1
John Leschinski
INDUSTRY: Design
AGENCY: Leschinski Design
LOCATION: Toronto, Ontario,
Canada

2
And Company
INDUSTRY: Public Relations
AGENCY: LSDspace
LOCATION: Madrid, Spain

3
Bytware
INDUSTRY: Technology
AGENCY: Stellar Debris
LOCATION: Hadano, Kanagawa
Japan

4
Susan Oldrid Interiors
INDUSTRY: Interior Design
AGENCY: Roskelly Inc.
LOCATION: Portsmouth, RI

1

2

1
Ann Bell Alford
INDUSTRY: Classical Singer /
Vocal Coach
AGENCY: DogStar Design
LOCATION: Birmingham, AL

2
**Alabama Symphony
Orchestra**
INDUSTRY: Fund Raising
AGENCY: DogStar Design
LOCATION: Birmingham, AL

1

2

3

4

1

McDevitt & Newman
INDUSTRY: Community Service
AGENCY: McMillian Design
LOCATION: Brooklyn, NY

2

**Creation Care, Solana
Beach Presbyterian Church**
INDUSTRY: Religion
AGENCY: Church Logo Gallery
LOCATION: Oceanside, CA

3

Freedom Dairy Inc.
INDUSTRY: Dairy Production
AGENCY: Compass Creative
Studio
LOCATION: Burlington, Ontario
Canada

4

San Francisco Parks Trust
INDUSTRY: Nation Parks
Preservation & Management
AGENCY: MINE™
LOCATION: San Francisco, CA

1
Environmental Construction
INDUSTRY: Landscaping
AGENCY: McBreen Design, Inc.
LOCATION: Seattle, WA

2
Fresh & Spice
INDUSTRY: Fruit & Spice
Import-Export
AGENCY: Kenneth Diseño
LOCATION: Uruapan,
Michoacan, Mexico

3
Griffin + McGrath Irrigation
INDUSTRY: Irrigation Systems
AGENCY: Felt Design Group
LOCATION: Costa Mesa, CA

4
Agraria Farmers & Fishers
INDUSTRY: Restaurant
AGENCY: ripe.com
LOCATION: Washington, DC

Ecology Center
INDUSTRY: Environmental
Organization
AGENCY: D&Dre Creative
LOCATION: Round Rock, TX

1

2

1

Ecology Center / Forest Division

INDUSTRY: Environmental Organization
AGENCY: D&Dre Creative
LOCATION: Round Rock, TX

2

Ecology Center / Coastal Division

INDUSTRY: Environmental Organization
AGENCY: D&Dre Creative
LOCATION: Round Rock, TX

1

2

3

4

1

Devon Energy
INDUSTRY: Natural Gas
& Oil Production
AGENCY: Devon
LOCATION: Oklahoma City, OK

2

Trivia Kingdom
INDUSTRY: Games /
Entertainment
AGENCY: Roskelly Inc.
LOCATION: Portsmouth, RI

3

ANK Recordings
INDUSTRY: Music
AGENCY: XYARTS
LOCATION: Braeside, Victoria,
Australia

4

Hi-Dose Concreters
INDUSTRY: Construction
AGENCY: XYARTS
LOCATION: Braeside, Victoria,
Australia

1

2

3

4

1
Devon Energy
INDUSTRY: Natural Gas
& Oil Production
AGENCY: Devon
LOCATION: Oklahoma City, OK

2
CFP
INDUSTRY: Wine
AGENCY: Studio GT&P
LOCATION: Foligno, Italy

3
Scientific Arts
INDUSTRY: Design
AGENCY: XYARTS
LOCATION: Braeside, Victoria,
Australia

4
Tao Living
INDUSTRY: Lifestyle / Health
AGENCY: Logoholik
LOCATION: Belgrade, Serbia

1

2

1
Element 74
INDUSTRY: Website Design
AGENCY: Allison Lent
LOCATION: Columbia, MO

2
Pratt & Whitney
INDUSTRY: Technology /
Manufacturing
AGENCY: Bertz Design Group
LOCATION: Middletown, CT

1

2

1
**Alabama Symphony
Orchestra**
INDUSTRY: Symphony
Orchestra
AGENCY: DogStar Design
LOCATION: Birmingham, AL

2
Whirlpool
INDUSTRY: Retail
AGENCY: Bronson Ma Creative
LOCATION: San Antonio, TX

1

2

3

1

Betty Moyer
INDUSTRY: Stage & Film Actress
AGENCY: Oakley Design Studios
LOCATION: Portland, OR

2

Flashbg.org
INDUSTRY: Web Portal
AGENCY: Odigy
LOCATION: Brunei Darussalam

3

**Innovative Beverage
Concepts, Inc.**
INDUSTRY: Beverage
AGENCY: Mary Hutchison
Design, LLC
LOCATION: Seattle, WA

1

2

3

1

Eddie Bauer

INDUSTRY: Apparel & Outdoor Gear

AGENCY: Weather Control

LOCATION: Seattle, WA

2

American Heart Association Heart Ball Gala

INDUSTRY: Non Profit

AGENCY: Clockwork Studios

LOCATION: San Antonio, TX

3

Borres Productions

INDUSTRY: Film Production Company

AGENCY: Jack Tom Design

LOCATION: Bridgeport, CT

1

**Commissioner of Official
Languages for New Brunswick**
INDUSTRY: Government
AGENCY: Razor Creative
LOCATION: Moncton,
New Brunswick, Canada

2

Qualys, Inc.
INDUSTRY: Network Security
AGENCY: Gee + Chung Design
LOCATION: San Francisco, CA

3

Kerr Drug
INDUSTRY: Retail
AGENCY: Fifth Letter
LOCATION: Winston-Salem, NC

4

ScreeNerd.com
INDUSTRY: Internet
AGENCY: ohTwentyone
LOCATION: Colleyville, TX

1

2

3

4

1

Self-Promotion
INDUSTRY: Religion
AGENCY: Grace Fellowship
Church
LOCATION: Snellville, GA

2

Justin Winget
INDUSTRY: Graphic Design
AGENCY: Levy Restaurants
LOCATION: Chicago, IL

3

The Manitowoc Bandits
INDUSTRY: Sports
AGENCY: Levy Restaurants
LOCATION: Chicago, IL

4

Bremerton High School
INDUSTRY: Athletics / Sports
AGENCY: Niedermeier Design
LOCATION: Seattle, WA

1

2

3

1
Self-Promotion
INDUSTRY: Graphic Design
AGENCY: The Greater Good
Design
LOCATION: St. Cloud, FL

2
**The Hudner Oncology
Center**
INDUSTRY: Hospital
AGENCY: Roskelly Inc.
LOCATION: Portsmouth, RI

3
Self-Promotion
INDUSTRY: Church
AGENCY: Grace Fellowship
Church
LOCATION: Snellville, GA

1

2

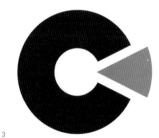

3

1
Content Genie
INDUSTRY: Furniture
Restoration
AGENCY: Blackbooks
LOCATION: Ft. Lauderdale, FL

2
Comunitat Valenciana
INDUSTRY: Tourism
AGENCY: LSDspace
LOCATION: Madrid, Spain

3
Capital Community Fund
INDUSTRY: Financial
AGENCY: Jack Tom Design
LOCATION: Bridgeport, CT

1

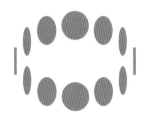

2

3

4

1

Conversay
INDUSTRY: Voice Recognition
AGENCY: Niedermeier Design
LOCATION: Seattle, WA

2

**Art Center College of
Design Alumni Council**
INDUSTRY: Education
AGENCY: Gee + Chung Design
LOCATION: San Francisco, CA

3

Net Medika
INDUSTRY: Global Medical
Services
AGENCY: LSDspace
LOCATION: Madrid, Spain

4

Humanity+
INDUSTRY: Technology
AGENCY: MINE™
LOCATION: San Francisco, CA

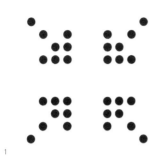

1

2

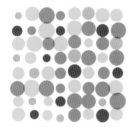

3

4

1
Medical Error Reduction Program
INDUSTRY: Medical
AGENCY: 3 Advertising
LOCATION: Albuquerque, NM

2
Accensible
INDUSTRY: Software
AGENCY: Niedermeier Design
LOCATION: Seattle, WA

3
Open Square
INDUSTRY: Grant Making
AGENCY: MINE™
LOCATION: San Francisco, CA

4
Dr. Zoran Dindjic Foundation
INDUSTRY: Nonprofit Education
AGENCY: Mirko Ilic Corp
LOCATION: New York, NY

1

2

3

1

Office Angels
INDUSTRY: Office Assistant
Service
AGENCY: D&Dre Creative
LOCATION: Round Rock, TX

2

NIRI
INDUSTRY: Networking
AGENCY: Riley Designs
LOCATION: Basalt, CO

3

SeeSlim Sportswear
INDUSTRY: Sportswear
AGENCY: LEBOW
LOCATION: Toronto, Ontario,
Canada

1

2

3

1
Shawn Lynch
INDUSTRY: Podcasting
AGENCY: Fifth Letter
LOCATION: Winston-Salem, NC

2
Monterey Bay Wine Company
INDUSTRY: Wine
AGENCY: Design Source Creative, Inc.
LOCATION: Aptos, CA

3
Paradoxy Products
INDUSTRY: Novelty Items
AGENCY: Mirko Ilic Corp
LOCATION: New York, NY

1

2

3

4

1
Lowertown Lofts
INDUSTRY: Real Estate
Development
AGENCY: Scott Adams
Design Associates
LOCATION: Minneapolis, MN

2
Andrej Kos
INDUSTRY: Winegrower
AGENCY: Krog
LOCATION: Ljubljana, Slovenia

3
Rattlecan Films
INDUSTRY: Entertainment
AGENCY: Moxie Sozo
LOCATION: Boulder, CO

4
Adam
INDUSTRY: Greeting Cards
& Stationary Products
AGENCY: Scott Adams
Design Associates
LOCATION: Minneapolis, MN

**The Potter League for
Animals**
INDUSTRY: Animal Shelter
AGENCY: Roskelly Inc.
LOCATION: Portsmouth, RI

1

2

3

4

1
Alert! Atlanta
INDUSTRY: Human Rights
AGENCY: Allen Creative
LOCATION: Snellville, GA

2
**New Providence
Memorial Library**
INDUSTRY: Education
AGENCY: Creative Madhouse
LOCATION: Fort Worth, TX

3
Poet
INDUSTRY: Alternative Energy
AGENCY: 3 Advertising
LOCATION: Albuquerque, NM

4
**Screen Door Open
Charity Golf**
INDUSTRY: Nonprofit
AGENCY: Bronson Ma Creative
LOCATION: San Antonio, TX

1

2

3

4

1	2	3	4
Robertson Controls • Electric	**BITS**	**Meyer Projection Systems**	**Minerva**
INDUSTRY: Manufacturing	INDUSTRY: Technology	INDUSTRY: Film & Video	INDUSTRY: Antiquities Dealer
AGENCY: Cellar Door Creative	AGENCY: Burn Creative	AGENCY: Oakley Design Studios	AGENCY: Niedermeier Design
LOCATION: Oak Park, IL	LOCATION: Carlisle, PA	LOCATION: Portland, OR	LOCATION: Seattle, WA

1

2

3

4

1
Two
INDUSTRY: Design
AGENCY: Stefan Romanu
LOCATION: Timisoara, Romania

2
Self-Promotion
INDUSTRY: Graphic Design
AGENCY: ELLIOT
LOCATION: Montreal, Quebec,
Canada

3
Lluís M. García
INDUSTRY: Blog
AGENCY: Fran Rosa Soler
LOCATION: Spain

4
Local.com
INDUSTRY: Internet
AGENCY: Ramp
Creative+Design
LOCATION: Los Angeles, CA

1

2

3

4

1
Vanessa Blair
INDUSTRY: Real Estate
AGENCY: Rebekah Albrecht
Graphic Design
LOCATION: Los Angeles, CA

2
Medi Didac
INDUSTRY: Health Education
AGENCY: Q
LOCATION: Wiesbaden,
Germany

3
CyberNet Entertainment
INDUSTRY: Entertainment
AGENCY: MINE™
LOCATION: San Francisco, CA

4
HighWire
INDUSTRY: Publishing
AGENCY: MINE™
LOCATION: San Francisco, CA

**The Steppin' For A Cure
Breast Cancer 3-Day Team**
INDUSTRY: Non-profit
AGENCY: Creative Madhouse
LOCATION: Fort Worth, TX

1

2

3

4

1

Angela

INDUSTRY: Massage Therapy
AGENCY: Oakley Design Studios
LOCATION: Portland, OR

2

Sogemap Inc.

INDUSTRY: Evaluation of
Government Programs
AGENCY: Subcommunication
LOCATION: Montreal, Quebec,
Canada

3

Self-Promotion

INDUSTRY: Graphic Design
AGENCY: DavidPCrawford.com
LOCATION: Pittsburgh, PA

4

John McDermott

INDUSTRY: Photography
AGENCY: Neil T McDonald
LOCATION: Glasgow,
Lanarkshire, U.K.

1

2

3

4

1
LaunchPad
INDUSTRY: Web Development
AGENCY: Squarelogo Design
LOCATION: Lakeville, MN

2
Cancer Sell
INDUSTRY: Non-profit
AGENCY: Stefan Romanu
LOCATION: Timisoara, Romania

3
LEAF Eco-Advocacy Foundation
INDUSTRY: Hospitality
Eco-Advocacy Foundation
AGENCY: ripe.com
LOCATION: Washington, DC

4
Coffee Bean & Tea Leaf
INDUSTRY: Food/Beverage
AGENCY: Hornall Anderson
LOCATION: Seattle, WA

1

2

3

4

1
ITP International
INDUSTRY: Self-Help
AGENCY: MINE™
LOCATION: San Francisco, CA

2
The Art of Peace Foundation
INDUSTRY: Non-Profit
AGENCY: ripe.com
LOCATION: Washington, DC

3
Helga
INDUSTRY: Language Learning Centre
AGENCY: Graphic Design Studio by Yurko Gutsulyak
LOCATION: Kyiv, Ukraine

4
CBS Radio • Kink FM
INDUSTRY: Music
AGENCY: Oakley Design Studios
LOCATION: Portland, OR

1

2

3

4

1
La Ilusion Orchards
INDUSTRY: Agriculture
AGENCY: Kenneth Diseño
LOCATION: Uruapan,
Michoacan, Mexico

2
**Bridgeport
Neighborhood Trust**
INDUSTRY: Housing Program
Developer
AGENCY: Jack Tom Design
LOCATION: Bridgeport, CT

3
Tomas Martinez Architect
INDUSTRY: Architecture
AGENCY: LSDspace
LOCATION: Madrid, Spain

4
Modus Propane
INDUSTRY: Utilities
AGENCY: Reactor, LLC
LOCATION: Kansas City, MO

1

2

3

1
**T Communications &
Community**
INDUSTRY: IT
AGENCY: Tinged
LOCATION: Makati, Philippines

2
Vox Verde
INDUSTRY: Advertising
& Consulting
AGENCY: Logoholik
LOCATION: Belgrade, Serbia

3
Powerwall Solutions
INDUSTRY: Construction
AGENCY: XYARTS
LOCATION: Braeside, Victoria,
Australia

1

2

3

1
Harvest Pest Control
INDUSTRY: Pest Control
AGENCY: D&Dre Creative
LOCATION: Round Rock, TX

2
Steve Ford Music
INDUSTRY: Music Studio for
the Advertising Industry
AGENCY: DogStar Design
LOCATION: Birmingham, AL

3
**Parasite Control
Wiesbaden**
INDUSTRY: Pest Control
AGENCY: Q
LOCATION: Wiesbaden,
Germany

1

2

3

4

1
Japan Germany Forum
INDUSTRY: Student Exchange
Program
AGENCY: Paul Snowden
LOCATION: Berlin, Germany

2
DirectColor
INDUSTRY: Printing
AGENCY: Ramp
Creative+Design
LOCATION: Los Angeles, CA

3
X-BAR
INDUSTRY: IT Consultancy
AGENCY: Niedermeier Design
LOCATION: Seattle, WA

4
Self-Promotion
INDUSTRY: Graphic Design
AGENCY: Daniel Green
Eye-D Design
LOCATION: Green Bay, WI

1

2

1
Nielsen Real Estate Sales
INDUSTRY: Real Estate
AGENCY: Niedermeier Design
LOCATION: Seattle, WA

2
Solutions in Software
INDUSTRY: Technology
AGENCY: Bronson Ma Creative
LOCATION: San Antonio, TX

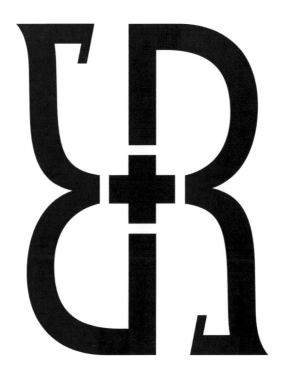

Emergency Room

INDUSTRY: Design
AGENCY: NP Graphic Design
LOCATION: Simsbury, CT

1

2

3

4

1	2	3	4
Tradesinfo.ca	**Sourcing Factory**	**Yacht**	**Prominic.NET, Inc.**
INDUSTRY: Education	INDUSTRY: Procurement	INDUSTRY: Music	INDUSTRY: Web hosting
AGENCY: Logoholik	AGENCY: Logoholik	AGENCY: Ian Lynam Creative Direction & Graphic Design	AGENCY: Hexanine
LOCATION: Belgrade, Serbia	LOCATION: Belgrade, Serbia	LOCATION: Toyko, Japan	LOCATION: Chicago, IL

1

2

3

4

1
**Scout Service Group /
Running**
INDUSTRY: Clothing & Apparel
AGENCY: D&Dre Creative
LOCATION: Round Rock, TX

2
Scout Service Group / Yoga
INDUSTRY: Clothing & Apparel
AGENCY: D&Dre Creative
LOCATION: Round Rock, TX

3
**Scout Service Group /
Tennis**
INDUSTRY: Clothing & Apparel
AGENCY: D&Dre Creative
LOCATION: Round Rock, TX

4
**Scout Service Group /
Snowboarding**
INDUSTRY: Clothing & Apparel
AGENCY: D&Dre Creative
LOCATION: Round Rock, TX

1

2

3

4

1
Defense Media Activity
INDUSTRY: Military
AGENCY: Niedermeier Design
LOCATION: Seattle, WA

2
Bud˙ Laska
INDUSTRY: Insurance
AGENCY: Graphic Design
Studio by Yurko Gutsulyak
LOCATION: Kyiv, Ukraine

3
Optimum Energy Company
INDUSTRY: HVAC systems
AGENCY: McBreen Design, Inc.
LOCATION: Seattle, WA

4
**Center for Cognitive
Computing**
INDUSTRY: Technology
AGENCY: MINE™
LOCATION: San Francisco, CA

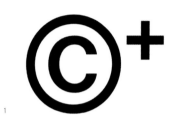

1

2

3

4

1
C Plus Jewelry
INDUSTRY: Jewelry
AGENCY: MINE™
LOCATION: San Francisco, CA

2
InterCity Security
INDUSTRY: Home Alarms
AGENCY: Roskelly Inc.
LOCATION: Portsmouth, RI

3
**Asociacion Cameristica
Española**
INDUSTRY: Classical Music
AGENCY: LSDspace
LOCATION: Madrid, Spain

4
Laura Burns Gericke
INDUSTRY: Social Networking
AGENCY: Designlab, Inc.
LOCATION: St. Louis, MO

1

2

1
Taxiarches
INDUSTRY: Religion
AGENCY: XYARTS
LOCATION: Braeside, Victoria,
Australia

2
Auto MotorPlex
Minneapolis
INDUSTRY: Motorsports Club
AGENCY: Squarelogo Design
LOCATION: Lakeville, MN

1

2

1
Visual Temptations Only
INDUSTRY: Garment
AGENCY: Masood Bukhari
LOCATION: Bronx, NY

2
Media Masters
INDUSTRY: Communications
AGENCY: Solak Design Co.
LOCATION: New Hartford, CT

1

2

3

4

1

**Acorn Park Nursery
& Kindergarten, Ltd.**
INDUSTRY: Childcare
AGENCY: Neil T McDonald
LOCATION: Glasgow,
Lanarkshire, UK

2

SLNS
INDUSTRY: Fashion
AGENCY: Neil T McDonald
LOCATION: Glasgow,
Lanarkshire, UK

3

The Seeing Eye
INDUSTRY: Non-Profit
AGENCY: Hames Design
LOCATION: Mohegan Lake, NY

4

**Northeast Dallas
Chamber of Commerce**
INDUSTRY: Professional
Services
AGENCY: Bronson Ma Creative
LOCATION: San Antonio, TX

1

2

3

4

1

Patricia Glaser
INDUSTRY: Personal Chef
AGENCY: Roskelly Inc.
LOCATION: Portsmouth, RI

2

Sea of Silver
INDUSTRY: Silver Jewelry Retail
AGENCY: AkarStudios
LOCATION: Santa Monica, CA

3

**Dentonia Park
Capital Management**
INDUSTRY: Financial
AGENCY: Remo Strada Design
LOCATION: Lincroft, NJ

4

Majores Painting
INDUSTRY: Painting
AGENCY: XYARTS
LOCATION: Braeside,
Victoria, Australia

1

2

3

1
International Spy Museum
INDUSTRY: Museum
AGENCY: MBCreative
LOCATION: Denton, TX

2
Grace Fellowship Church
INDUSTRY: Religion
AGENCY: Grace Fellowship
Church
LOCATION: Snellville, GA

3
Clearstory
INDUSTRY: Real Estate
AGENCY: Maycreate Idea
Group
LOCATION: Chattanooga, TN

1

2

3

4

1

Camera di Commercio Italiana
INDUSTRY: Commerce Chamber
AGENCY: Stefan Romanu
LOCATION: Timisoara, Romania

2

Islamic Library Studies & Charitable Trust
INDUSTRY: Charitable Library
AGENCY: Storm Corporate Design
LOCATION: Auckland, New Zealand

3

Ediciones Tenacitas
INDUSTRY: Publishing
AGENCY: LSDspace
LOCATION: Madrid, Spain

4

Guck Boats
INDUSTRY: Marine Boat Builder
AGENCY: Roskelly Inc.
LOCATION: Portsmouth, RI

1

2

3

1

Self-Promotion

INDUSTRY: Graphic Design

AGENCY: Urban Influence

LOCATION: Seattle, WA

2

Self-Promotion

INDUSTRY: Illustration

AGENCY: Diversified Apparel

LOCATION: Toledo, OH

3

Susquehanna University

INDUSTRY: Education

AGENCY: MFDI

LOCATION: Selinsgrove, PA

1

2

3

1

Jennifer R. A. Campbell
INDUSTRY: Fine Artist/Painter
AGENCY: idAPostle
LOCATION: Ottawa, Alberta,
Canada

2

Andrew Young & Co
INDUSTRY: Hospitality
AGENCY: Mirko Ilic Corp.
LOCATION: New York, NY

3

**Alabama Symphony
Volunteer Council**
INDUSTRY: Non-Profit
AGENCY: DogStar Design
LOCATION: Birmingham, AL

1

2

3

4

1

Music Saves

INDUSTRY: Music Retail

AGENCY: Little Jacket

LOCATION: Cleveland, OH

2

MyDJSpace.net

INDUSTRY: Entertainment

AGENCY: Logoholik

LOCATION: Belgrade, Serbia

3

Hey, Hot Shot!

INDUSTRY: Photography
competition

AGENCY: Little Jacket

LOCATION: Cleveland, OH

4

**Museum of the History
of Yugoslavia (MIJ)**

INDUSTRY: Museum

AGENCY: Mirko Ilic Corp.

LOCATION: New York, NY

1

2

3

4

1
The Stables at Millennium
INDUSTRY: Real Estate
AGENCY: Roskelly Inc.
LOCATION: Portsmouth, RI

2
Local Hooker Rods
INDUSTRY: Fishing
AGENCY: Roskelly Inc.
LOCATION: Portsmouth, RI

3
Pizza Plus
INDUSTRY: Food & Beverage
AGENCY: Roskelly Inc.
LOCATION: Portsmouth, RI

4
Soundview Medical
INDUSTRY: Home Care
Medical Supplies
AGENCY: Niedermeier Design
LOCATION: Seattle, WA

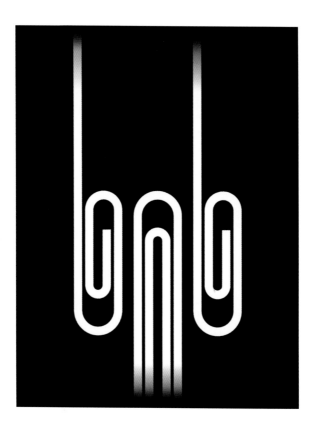

BNB
INDUSTRY: Retail Office
Equipment
AGENCY: Stefan Romanu
LOCATION: Timisoara, Romania

1

2

3

4

1	2	3	4
Ediving Market	**Southern Seafood Suppliers, Inc.**	**Global Web Code**	**Sin Bichos**
INDUSTRY: Recreation	INDUSTRY: Wholesale Seafood Supplier	INDUSTRY: Web Services	INDUSTRY: Pest Control
AGENCY: LSDspace	AGENCY: Scott Ott Creative, Inc.	AGENCY: LSDspace	AGENCY: LSDspace
LOCATION: Madrid, Spain	LOCATION: New Orleans, LA	LOCATION: Madrid, Spain	LOCATION: Madrid, Spain

1

2

3

4

1
AEAS
INDUSTRY: Water Control
AGENCY: LSDspace
LOCATION: Madrid, Spain

2
Skyoflove.org
INDUSTRY: Non-Profit
AGENCY: Logoholik
LOCATION: Belgrade, Serbia

3
Al Aire Books
INDUSTRY: Publishing
AGENCY: LSDspace
LOCATION: Madrid, Spain

4
Sound Decision, Inc.
INDUSTRY: Custom Car Audio
AGENCY: Nickolas Narczewski
LOCATION: Plano, IL

1

2

3

4

1
Ero Kosova
INDUSTRY: Government
(Energy)
AGENCY: projectGRAPHICS.EU
LOCATION: Kosova, Albania

2
Reverse Mortgage Texas
INDUSTRY: Real Estate
AGENCY: Bronson Ma
LOCATION: San Antonio, TX

3
Birddy
INDUSTRY: Write
AGENCY: LSDspace
LOCATION: Madrid, Spain

4
Doorcats
INDUSTRY: Doors and
Windows
AGENCY: LSDspace
LOCATION: Madrid, Spain

1

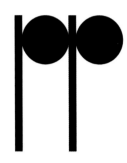

3

2

1

Pilotprojekt Gallery
INDUSTRY: Design Gallery
AGENCY: Alexander Egger
LOCATION: Vienna, AL

2

Burgweid
INDUSTRY: Real Estate
AGENCY: Masood Bukhari
LOCATION: Bronx, NY

3

Tihany Design
INDUSTRY: Interior Design /
Architecture
AGENCY: Mirko Ilic Corp
LOCATION: New York, NY

1

2

3

4

1
Art Guard
INDUSTRY: Electronics
AGENCY: Frank D'Astolfo
Design
LOCATION: Willow, NY

2
Andrej Mlakar
INDUSTRY: Architect
AGENCY: Krog
LOCATION: Ljubljana, Slovenia

3
B&Beyond Apparel
INDUSTRY: Apparel
AGENCY: Ramp
Creative+Design
LOCATION: Los Angeles, CA

4
Niedermeier Design
INDUSTRY: Graphic Design
AGENCY: Niedermeier Design
LOCATION: Seattle, WA

1

2

3

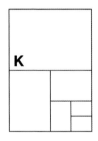

4

1
GenMobi Technologies
INDUSTRY: Fraud Protection
AGENCY: Mariana Pabon
LOCATION: San Francisco, CA

2
Hasaj
INDUSTRY: Dentist
AGENCY: Krog
LOCATION: Ljubljana, Slovenia

3
Go Maganize
INDUSTRY: Publishing
AGENCY: Tangent Graphic
LOCATION: Glasgow,
Lanarkshire, UK

4
Krungthep Architecture
INDUSTRY: Architecture
AGENCY: Ian Lynam Creative
Direction & Graphic Design
LOCATION: Tokyo, Japan

1

2

3

1
Prairie Egg Distributors
INDUSTRY: Dairy Distributor
AGENCY: D&Dre Creative
LOCATION: Round Rock, TX

2
Higland Baptist Church
INDUSTRY: Non Profit
AGENCY: Bronson Ma Creative
LOCATION: San Antonio, TX

3
Mirtille
INDUSTRY: Fast Casual Dining
AGENCY: AkarStudios
LOCATION: Santa Monica, CA

WORDMARKS

1

2

3

4

1	2	3	4
Eddie Bauer	**Presh**	**Zumiez**	**Pipeline**
INDUSTRY: Apparel	INDUSTRY: Jewelry	INDUSTRY: Sports Apparel	INDUSTRY: Non-profit
AGENCY: Weather Control	AGENCY: UNIT Design	AGENCY: Weather Control	AGENCY: 3rd Edge
LOCATION: Seattle, WA	Collective	LOCATION: Seattle, WA	Communications
	LOCATION: San Francisco, CA		LOCATION: Jersey City, NJ

1

2

1
Brandi Carlile
INDUSTRY: Music
AGENCY: Weather Control
LOCATION: Seattle, WA

2
Anberlin
INDUSTRY: Music
AGENCY: Weather Control
LOCATION: Seattle, WA

Fuel Fitness
INDUSTRY: Fitness
AGENCY: Siah Design
LOCATION: Alberta, Canada

quest

1

2

LiQWd.

3

4

1
Quest
INDUSTRY: Advertising
AGENCY: Alex Mirea Creative
Studio
LOCATION: Hunedoara, Romania

2
Geek Monthly Magazine
INDUSTRY: Publishing
AGENCY: Hexanine
LOCATION: Chicago, IL

3
Olatherapy
INDUSTRY: Hair & Beauty
AGENCY: UNIT Design
Collective
LOCATION: San Francisco, CA

4
California Film Institute
INDUSTRY: Arts &
Entertainment
AGENCY: MINE™
LOCATION: San Francisco, CA

1

2

VETRO

3

undeGRAND

4

1

Wiser Skate Pro
INDUSTRY: Pro Skating
AGENCY: diografic
LOCATION: Lisbon, Portugal

2

Micro Films
INDUSTRY: Photo & Film
AGENCY: LSDspace
LOCATION: Madrid, Spain

3

Vetro
INDUSTRY: Book Exchange
AGENCY: diografic
LOCATION: Lisbon, Portugal

4

UnderGRAND
INDUSTRY: Night Club
AGENCY: Riverbed
LOCATION: Seattle, WA

ideothas

Andy Gore

1
Umbelino Monteiro
INDUSTRY: Ceramic Tile
Manufacturer
AGENCY: diografic
LOCATION: Lisbon, Portugal

2
Ruadesign
INDUSTRY: Design
AGENCY: diografic
LOCATION: Lisbon, Portugal

3
Triad Management Group
INDUSTRY: Management Group
AGENCY: diografic
LOCATION: Lisbon, Portugal

4
Uptown
INDUSTRY: Photography
AGENCY: Mabu
LOCATION: Fyn, Denmark

1

2

3

4

°123**W**EST°

FRIDAY HARBOR

1
Kvart
INDUSTRY: Publication
AGENCY: Mirko Ilic Corp
LOCATION: New York, NY

2
Red Loft
INDUSTRY: Regeneration &
Housing Development
AGENCY: Crumpled Dog
Design
LOCATION: London, UK

3
R3 R
INDUSTRY: Web Development
AGENCY: UNIT Design
Collective
LOCATION: San Francisco, CA

4
123 West
INDUSTRY: Housing
Development
AGENCY: Urban Influence
LOCATION: Seattle, WA

2

3

4

1
Rimi Baltic
INDUSTRY: Food
AGENCY: Daymon
Worldwide Design
LOCATION: Stamford, CT

2
Geneva Concours d' Elegance
INDUSTRY: Automotive
Showcase / Charity
AGENCY: Nickolas Narczewski
LOCATION: Plano, IL

3
**Noora's Mediterranean
Kitchen**
INDUSTRY: Restaurant
AGENCY: Storm Corporate Design
LOCATION: Auckland, New
Zealand

4
**Art Directors Club of New
Jersey**
INDUSTRY: Non-Profit
AGENCY: Ana Paula Rodrigues
Design
LOCATION: Newark, NJ

olbex

1

ENZOCREATIVE

2

ACETEC

3

aidasaracini

4

1
Olbex
INDUSTRY: Technology
AGENCY: Stressdesign
LOCATION: Syracuse, NY

2
Self-Promotion
INDUSTRY: Design
AGENCY: Enzo Creative
LCOATION: Summit, NJ

3
AceTec
INDUSTRY: Event Planning
AGENCY: Q
LOCATION: Wiesbaden,
Germany

4
Aida Saracini
INDUSTRY: Fashion Designer
AGENCY: projectGRAPHICS.EU
LOCATION: Prishtina, Kosova,
Albania

smarts^{TM}

1

INTERACTYX

2

CLARIMAX

3

ELITE=DITING

4

1
**The Vega Project
& WallCandy Arts**
INDUSTRY: Baby & Educational
Products / Wall Decor
AGENCY: The Vega Project
LOCATION: San Francisco, CA

2
Interactyx
INDUSTRY: Learning Center
AGENCY: ArtVersion
LOCATION: Northfield, IL

3
Clarimax
INDUSTRY: Consumer Products
AGENCY: Q
LOCATION: Wiesbaden,
Germany

4
Elite Editing
INDUSTRY: Editing
AGENCY: DavidPCrawford.com
LOCATION: Pittsburgh, PA

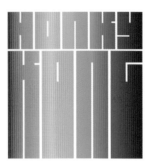

1

2

1
Honky Kong
INDUSTRY: Apparel
AGENCY: Ian Lynam Creative
Direction & Graphic Design
LOCATION: Tokyo, Japan

2
Self-Promotion
INDUSTRY: Communication
Design
AGENCY: NalinDesign
LOCATION: Neuenrade, Germany

Munchkin®

INDUSTRY: Baby & Childcare Products

AGENCY: The UXB

LOCATION: Beverly Hills, CA

1

2

3

4

1
Mojo Club
INDUSTRY: Night Club
AGENCY: Alex Mirea Creative
Studio
LOCATION: Hunedoara, Romania

2
Point Line Plane
INDUSTRY: Music
AGENCY: Ian Lynam Creative
Direction & Graphic Design
LOCATION: Tokyo, Japan

3
Nordique Music
INDUSTRY: Music
AGENCY: Subcommunication
LOCATION: Quebec, Canada

4
NOON
INDUSTRY: Design
AGENCY: Neil T McDonald
LOCATION: Lanarkshire, UK

exposed

Dan Sidor
PHOTOGRAPHY

1
Exposed
INDUSTRY: Clothing Boutique
AGENCY: Rebecca Carroll
LOCATION: Nashville, TN

2
Print Brigade
INDUSTRY: Fashion
AGENCY: Chris Piascik
LOCATION: Cambridge, MA

3
Character Bags
INDUSTRY: Fashion
AGENCY: Kalico Design
LOCATION: Frederick, MD

4
Dan Sidor Photography
INDUSTRY: Commercial
Photography
AGENCY: Honest Bros.
LOCATION: Denver, CO

1

2

Fotografia

3

4

1
**Museo Arqueologico
de Murcia**
INDUSTRY: Museum
AGENCY: LSDspace
LOCATION: Madrid, Spain

2
Nexus Imaging
INDUSTRY: Photography
AGENCY: Storm Corporate
Design
LOCATION: Auckland,
New Zealand

3
FG Press
INDUSTRY: Photography
AGENCY: mabu
LOCATION: Fyn, Denmark

4
Fino
INDUSTRY: Food Importer
AGENCY: MINE™
LOCATION: San Francisco, CA

NORTHSEA CAPITAL

1

2

3

WHITEFRIARS

CANTERBURY

4

1
Northsea Capital
INDUSTRY: Private Equity
AGENCY: We Recommend
LOCATION: Copenhagen, Denmark

2
LIKELIFE Records
INDUSTRY: Music
AGENCY: Oakley Design Studios
LOCATION: Portland, OR

3
The Arboretum of South Barrington
INDUSTRY: Shopping Center
AGENCY: Ten26 Design Group, Inc.
LOCATION: Crystal Lake, IL

4
Land Securities
INDUSTRY: Real Estate
AGENCY: Nextbigthing
LOCATION: London, UK

LOKALT
SVENSKT
NÄRINGSLIV
SKÅNE
HALLAND
BLEKINGE
FÖRETAGSKLIMAT

Svenskt Näringsliv

INDUSTRY: Business
Development
AGENCY: We Recommend
LOCATION: Copenhagen,
Denmark

1

2

3

1
Fair Food Foundation
INDUSTRY: Nonprofit
AGENCY: BBMG
LOCATION: New York, NY

2
Hunter
INDUSTRY: Non-Profit
AGENCY: Doner
LOCATION: Cleveland, OH

3
Power Fuzz Clothing
INDUSTRY: Apparel
AGENCY: Weather Control
LOCATION: Seattle, WA

1

2

3

1
AC Printing Company
INDUSTRY: Printing
AGENCY: Reactor, LLC
LOCATION: Kansas City, MO

2
Pat Flavin
INDUSTRY: Real Estate
AGENCY: Miller Meiers Design
for Communication
LOCATION: Lawrence, KS

3
Vivio World
INDUSTRY: Creative Studio
AGENCY: InsaneFacilities
LOCATION: Lodz, Poland

1

2

3

4

1
**Carol & John's Comic
Book Shop**
INDUSTRY: Comic Book Shop
AGENCY: Little Jacket
LOCATION: Cleveland, OH

2
StyleBoston
INDUSTRY: TV Program
AGENCY: Alphabet Arm
LOCATION: Boston, MA

3
Self-Promotion
INDUSTRY: Design
AGENCY: Weather Control
LOCATION: Seattle, WA

3
Wordplay
INDUSTRY: Copywriting
AGENCY: Thinkhaus
LOCATION: Richmond, VA

tacksales

1

twotree
INTERNATIONAL

2

cíf
COMMUNITY INVESTMENT FUTURES

3

1
Tacksales Ltd.
INDUSTRY: Fashion
AGENCY: Entz Creative
LOCATION: Singapore

2
Two Tree International LLC
INDUSTRY: Product Design
AGENCY: Entz Creative
LOCATION: Singapore

3
CIF
INDUSTRY: Non Profit
AGENCY: Clockwork Studios
LOCATION: San Antonio, TX

Dig Trees, LLC
INDUSTRY: Agriculture /
Landscaping
AGENCY: Orange Bike Design
LOCATION: Los Angeles, CA

1

2

3

4

1
Jabbsaft Booking
INDUSTRY: Booking Agency
AGENCY: UREDD
LOCATION: Trondheim, Norway

2
Fluoro
INDUSTRY: Magazine
AGENCY: Housemouse
LOCATION: Victoria, Australia

3
Rossignol
INDUSTRY: Apparel
AGENCY: Weather Control
LOCATION: Seattle, WA

4
Zumiez
INDUSTRY: Apparel
AGENCY: Weather Control
LOCATION: Seattle, WA

1

Ray Charles

2

Parliament

3

liquorice

4

1
Fever Films North America
INDUSTRY: Film & Television
AGENCY: Ian Lynam Creative
Direction & Graphic Design
LOCATION: Tokyo, Japan

2
Patrick Lamb Productions
INDUSTRY: Music
AGENCY: Oakley Design
Studios
LOCATION: Portland, OR

3
Self-Promotion
INDUSTRY: Interactive Design
AGENCY: Parliament
LOCATION: Portland, OR

3
Darrell Lea
INDUSTRY: Confectionery
AGENCY: The Saltmine
LOCATION: Sydney, Australia

kooture

1

2

3

1

Kooture

INDUSTRY: Apparel

AGENCY: Ocular Ink

LOCATION: Nashville, TN

2

Self-Promotion

INDUSTRY: Design

AGENCY: BLVD Design Studio

LOCATION: New York, NY

3

Mundico

INDUSTRY: Various

AGENCY: Daniel Rothier

LOCATION: Rio de Janeiro, Brazil

1

2

3

4

1
World Transhumanist Association
INDUSTRY: Advanced Applied Science
AGENCY: MINE™
LOCATION: San Francisco, CA

2
Companion Baking
INDUSTRY: Food / Restaurant
AGENCY: Designlab, Inc.
LOCATION: St. Louis, MO

3
Self-Promotion
INDUSTRY: Graphic Design
AGENCY: Tracey Ortolano
LOCATION: New York, NY

4
VNU
INDUSTRY: Sports Team for Publisher
AGENCY: Ana Paula Rodrigues Design
LOCATION: Newark, NJ

1

2

3

4

1
Pink Swirl Chocolates
INDUSTRY: Food
AGENCY: Ten26 Design Group,
Inc.
LOCATION: Crystal Lake, IL

2
**The Mansion
at Maple Heights**
INDUSTRY: Event Venue
AGENCY: Design Intervention
LOCATION: Pittsburgh, PA

3
Phillips Communications
INDUSTRY: PR / Communications
AGENCY: Roskelly Inc.
LOCATION: Portsmouth, RI

4
LittleBlackbird
INDUSTRY: Retail
AGENCY: LogoManic
LOCATION: Ontario, Canada

OF THE MARTYR

1

2

1

Gesture Studios
INDUSTRY: Music
AGENCY: Honest Bros.
LOCATION: Denver, CO

2

Rock 'n' Roll Camp for Girls
INDUSTRY: Music Education
AGENCY: Plazm
LOCATION: Portland, OR

1

2

3

1
Barberella Hair Salon
INDUSTRY: Hair Salon
AGENCY: BigWig Design
LOCATION: San Francisco, CA

2
Pure Cuban Sugar
INDUSTRY: Music
AGENCY: Weather Control
LOCATION: Seattle, WA

3
Larry Skolnick
INDUSTRY: Food
AGENCY: Subcommunication
LOCATION: Montreal, Quebec, Canada

1

2

3

1
International Spy Museum
INDUSTRY: Museum
AGENCY: MBCreative
LOCATION: Denton, TX

2
Self-Promotion
INDUSTRY: Design
AGENCY: Weather Control
LOCATION: Seattle, WA

3
Go GaGa
INDUSTRY: Fashion
AGENCY: Alphabet Arm
LOCATION: Boston, MA

GCNU:NC

1

FACTORY

2

NOR⅃

3

OXC/\
LONDON

4

1
Genuine Advertising
INDUSTRY: Production facility
AGENCY: Stefan Romanu
LOCATION: Timisoara, Romania

2
Factory Creative Studio
INDUSTRY: Communication
Design
AGENCY: Stefan Romanu
LOCATION: Timisoara, Romania

3
Nord Proiect
INDUSTRY: Land Surveyor
AGENCY: Stefan Romanu
LOCATION: Timisoara, Romania

4
OCCA London
INDUSTRY: Fashion
AGENCY: Odigy
LOCATION: Brunei Darussalam

1

2

3

monopink

4

1
Rübik
INDUSTRY: Interior Design
AGENCY: Elliot
LOCATION: Montreal, QC
Canada

2
Carder & Associates
INDUSTRY: Consumer /
Manufacturing
AGENCY: Entz Creative
LOCATION: Singapore

3
Joshu + Vela
INDUSTRY: Apparel
AGENCY: Ian Lynam Creative
Direction & Graphic Design
LOCATION: Tokyo, Japan

4
Monopink
INDUSTRY: Design Studio
AGENCY: Q
LOCATION: Wiesbaden,
Germany

kollaborativ
media · marketing · consulting

1

maden

2

3

community
skate & snow

4

1
Kollaborative
INDUSTRY: Marketing
Consultation
AGENCY: Orange Bike Design
LOCATION: Los Angeles, CA

2
Maden Group
INDUSTRY: Magazine
AGENCY: projectGRAPHICS.EU
LOCATION: Prishtina, Kosova,
Albania

3
Food Machine
INDUSTRY: Fast Food
AGENCY: Storm Corporate
Design
LOCATION: Auckland,
New Zealand

4
Community Skate & Snow
INDUSTRY: Retail
AGENCY: Riverbed
LOCATION: Seattle, WA

1

MOODFOOD

2

CITY SPROUTS

3

1
Longview Equities, LLC
INDUSTRY: Real Estate
AGENCY: Imagebox
Productions, Inc.
LOCATION: Pittsburgh, PA

2
Moodfood Company
INDUSTRY: Retail Food
AGENCY: Tangent Graphic
LOCATION: Lanarkshire, UK

3
City Sprouts
INDUSTRY: Retail
AGENCY: Designlab, Inc.
LOCATION: St. Louis, MO

1

2

3

1
Cornerstones
INDUSTRY: Non-Profit
AGENCY: Maycreate
Idea Group
LOCATION: Chattanooga, TN

2
FrameCo, Inc.
INDUSTRY: Construction
AGENCY: Parallel Practice, LLC
LOCATION: Lakewood, OH

3
Riverview Baptist Church
INDUSTRY: Religion
AGENCY: Matcha Design
LOCATION: Tulsa, OK

LISINOCOR®

L I S I N O P R I L

1

WEMOTO

2

HEXAGINE

3

ONRAX

4

1
Osvah
INDUSTRY: Pharma Co
AGENCY: Mamordesign
LOCATION: Islamic Republic
of Iran

2
Wemoto
INDUSTRY: Fashion
AGENCY: Q
LOCATION: Wiesbaden,
Germany

3
Self-Promotion
INDUSTRY: Design
AGENCY: Hexanine
LOCATION: Chicago, IL

4
Onrax
INDUSTRY: Garage Storage /
Makeovers
AGENCY: Niedermeier Design
LOCATION: Seattle, WA

BLACKBOOKS

nedleary

PHOTOGRAPHY

pearl

1

Self-Promotion

INDUSTRY: Design &
Fabrication

AGENCY: Blackbooks

LOCATION: Ft. Lauderdale, FL

2

Ned Leary

INDUSTRY: Photography

AGENCY: Airtype Studio

LOCATION: Winston-Salem, MA

3

Self-Promotion

INDUSTRY: Hospitality

AGENCY: Levy Restaurants

LOCATION: Chicago, IL

Cuda Crazy
INDUSTRY: Classic Cars
AGENCY: LogoManic
LOCATION: Ontario, Canada

1

2

3

4

1
Zero Motorcycles
INDUSTRY: Electric Vehicles
AGENCY: Tread Creative
LOCATION: Los Gatos, CA

2
Plan8
INDUSTRY: Consulting
AGENCY: We Recommend
LOCATION: Copenhagen,
Denmark

3
Yikes
INDUSTRY: Apparel
AGENCY: Ian Lynam Creative
Direction & Graphic Design
LOCATION: Tokyo, Japan

4
Deep Nightclub
INDUSTRY: Outdoor Bar
AGENCY: Nils-Petter Edwalk
LOCATION: Sweden

1

2

3

4

1
Flaya
INDUSTRY: New Media Design
& Marketing Consulting
AGENCY: Foan82
LOCATION: Lisbon, Portugal

2
Kora Design Studio
INDUSTRY: Interior Design
AGENCY: Odigy
LOCATION: Brunei Darussalam

3
Self Promotion
INDUSTRY: Design
AGENCY: Uredd
LOCATION: Trondheim, Norway

4
Rimo
INDUSTRY: Car Tuning
AGENCY: Odigy
LOCATION: Brunei Darussalam

bubble tea & stuff

1

2

3

1
Tease
INDUSTRY: Food & Beverage
AGENCY: Langton Cherubino
Group
LOCATION: New York, NY

2
RUBB
INDUSTRY: Apparel
AGENCY: Talbot Design
Group, Inc.
LOCATION: Westlake Village, CA

3
Flojos
INDUSTRY: Footwear
AGENCY: Talbot Design
Group, Inc.
LOCATION: Westlake Village, CA

1

2

3

4

1
Designforum
INDUSTRY: Design
AGENCY: Alexander Egger
LOCATION: Vienna, Austria

2
Flow 33
INDUSTRY: Natural Health
Drinks
AGENCY: Danny Goldberg
Design
LOCATION: Tel Aviv, Israel

3
Slicejack.com
INDUSTRY: Web Development
AGENCY: Logoholik
LOCATION: Belgrade, Serbia

4
StraightSilly
INDUSTRY: Music
AGENCY: skinnyCorp /
Threadless
LOCATION: Chicago, IL

Slurkjuice™

Slurkcoffee™

1

magnetic
systems

2

B̄ENCHMARK
mortgage

3

1
Slurk
INDUSTRY: Food & Beverage
AGENCY: We Recommend
LOCATION: Copenhagen,
Denmark

2
Magnetic Systems
INDUSTRY: Technology
AGENCY: UNIT Design
Collective
LOCATION: San Francisco, CA

3
Benchmark Mortgage
INDUSTRY: Mortgage Company
AGENCY: YIU Studio
LOCATION: Seattle, WA

1

2

3

Scandinavian
Retail
Partner

4

1
The Gay Lesbian Center in Long Beach, CA
INDUSTRY: Non-Profit
AGENCY: Marc Posch Design, Inc.
LOCATION: Long Beach, CA

2
Ochs Center for Metropolitan Studies
INDUSTRY: Non-Profit
AGENCY: Maycreate Idea Group
LOCATION: Chattanooga, TN

3
BIL
INDUSTRY: Technology Conference
AGENCY: MINE™
LOCATION: San Francisco, CA

4
Scandinavian Retail Partner
INDUSTRY: Consulting
AGENCY: We Recommend
LOCATION: Copenhagen, Denmark

1

2

3

4

1
myJournal.com
INDUSTRY: Social/Business
Network
AGENCY: Sonet Digital
LOCATION: Bournemouth, UK

2
Nationwide Realty Investors
INDUSTRY: Real Estate
Development
AGENCY: Scott Adams Design
Associates
LOCATION: Minneapolis, MN

3
Amplify Her
INDUSTRY: Music
AGENCY: Roycroft Design
LOCATION: Boston, MA

4
Tunefisch
INDUSTRY: Music
AGENCY: Alexander Egger
LOCATION: Vienna, Austria

1

2

1
Frutier
INDUSTRY: Gourmet Foods
AGENCY: 2creativo
LOCATION: Barcelona, Spain

2
Open Hands Acupuncture
INDUSTRY: Acupuncture
AGENCY: Ian Lynam Creative
Direction & Graphic Design
LOCATION: Tokyo, Japan

grettasloane

1

2

solerelief

3

TRUE NORTH
CONSULTANTS

4

1
Gretta Sloane
INDUSTRY: Women's Apparel
AGENCY: Creative Squall
LOCATION: Trophy Club, TX

2
TruVision Pictures
INDUSTRY: Entertainment
AGENCY: KO11 Design
LOCATION: East Brunswick, NJ

3
Sole Relief
INDUSTRY: Footwear
AGENCY: Silver Creative Group
LOCATION: Norwalk, CT

4
True North Consultants
INDUSTRY: Engineering
AGENCY: Paper Tower
LOCATION: Elgin, IL

PHDINK

1
Eatastic Inc.
INDUSTRY: Social Networking
AGENCY: Entz Creative
LOCATION: Singapore

2
Salamificio Agrifood
INDUSTRY: Food
AGENCY: Studio GT&P
LOCATION: Foligno, Italy

3
First Cash Financial Services, Inc.
INDUSTRY: Financial
AGENCY: Creative Squall
LOCATION: Trophy Club, TX

4
PH Pink
INDUSTRY: Spa
AGENCY: Foan82
LOCATION: Lisbon, Portugal

ritualis

Ritualis
INDUSTRY: Unisex Beauty
Center
AGENCY: 2creativo
LOCATION: Barcelona, Spain

Phlip 'n' Nik
INDUSTRY: Food
AGENCY: Mariana Pabon
LOCATION: San Francisco, CA

1

2

3

{ **Kllapa** }

4

1
Juno Development
INDUSTRY: Development
AGENCY: Mirko Ilic Corp.
LOCATION: New York, NY

2
AIGA Philadelphia
INDUSTRY: Professional
Graphic Design Organization
AGENCY: Little Utopia, Inc.
LOCATION: Los Angeles, CA

3
Match Creative
INDUSTRY: Creative
Talent Agency
AGENCY: Geyrhalter Design
LOCATION: Santa Monica, CA

4
Kllapa
INDUSTRY: Web Portal
AGENCY: projectGRAPHICS.EU
LOCATION: Prishtina, Kosova,
Albania

1

2

3

4

1
Nurun
INDUSTRY: Internet
AGENCY: Design June
LOCATION: Montmorency,
France

2
Lost Magazine
INDUSTRY: Publishing
AGENCY: Ian Lynam Creative
Direction & Graphic Design
LOCATION: Tokyo, Japan

3
Gliese
INDUSTRY: Apparel
AGENCY: Foan82
LOCATION: Lisbon, Portugal

4
Rhoost
INDUSTRY: Child-Proofing
AGENCY: Alphabet Arm
LOCATION: Boston, MA

1

2

3

4

1
olx Studio Inc.
INDUSTRY: Architecture /
Product Design
AGENCY: Pryor Design
Company
LOCATION: Ann Arbor, MI

2
George Fontenette
INDUSTRY: Entertainment
AGENCY: 3rd Edge
Communications
LOCATION: Jersey City, NJ

3
Ix Tapa Cantina
INDUSTRY: Food / Restaurant
AGENCY: AkarStudios
LOCATION: Santa Monica, CA

4
Approved Appraisers
INDUSTRY: Home & Business
Appraisal
AGENCY: UNIT Design
Collective
LOCATION: San Francisco, CA

1

2

3

4

1
Fell Swoop
INDUSTRY: Digital Design
Consultant
AGENCY: YIU Studio
LOCATION: Seattle, WA

2
VoxStox
INDUSTRY: Online Political
Voting System
AGENCY: BBMG
LOCATION: New York, NY

3
Day One Fitness
INDUSTRY: Fitness
AGENCY: Ocular Ink
LOCATION: Nashville, TN

4
Conversation Agency
INDUSTRY: Marketing Agency
AGENCY: Geyrhalter Design
LOCATION: Santa Monica, CA

BRIGHTBRIDGE

1

BUSINESS ORCHARD

2

COBWEBMEDIA

3

CastRoller

4

1	2	3	4
Brightbridge	**Business Orchard**	**CobwebMedia**	**CastRoller**
INDUSTRY: Finance	INDUSTRY: Business Consultancy	INDUSTRY: Media Representative	INDUSTRY: Entertainment
AGENCY: Maycreate Idea Group	AGENCY: Nextbigthing	AGENCY: Krog	AGENCY: Leschinski Design
LOCATION: Chattanooga, TN	LOCATION: London, UK	LOCATION: Ljubljana, Slovenia	LOCATION: Toronto, ON, Canada

(ANSW3RS)

1

2

PERICON

UNTERNEHMENSBERATUNG

3

4

1
Huntington's Disease
Society of America
INDUSTRY: Non-Profit
AGENCY: Rizco Design
LOCATION: Manasquan, NJ

2
BlueFox Studio
INDUSTRY: Web Development
AGENCY: Entz Creative
LOCATION: Singapore

3
Pericon
INDUSTRY: Consulting
AGENCY: Q
LOCATION: Wiesbaden,
Germany

4
Holland America
INDUSTRY: Cruise
AGENCY: Hornall Anderson
LOCATION: Seattle, WA

1

2

1

Hair Eenvelope
INDUSTRY: Music
AGENCY: Weather Control
LOCATION: Seattle, WA

2

Eye Can Art
INDUSTRY: Kid's Toys
AGENCY: Weather Control
LOCATION: Seattle, WA

E D I (B) E R K

1

e l e v e n || s t a n w i x

2

3

LOOSE ENDS

4

1
Edi Berk
INDUSTRY: Design
AGENCY: Krog
LOCATION: Ljubljana, Slovenia

2
110 Gulf Associates of
Pittsburgh
INDUSTRY: Real-Estate
AGENCY: Kolano Design
LOCATION: Pittsburgh, PA

3
Darkwood Dub
INDUSTRY: Music
AGENCY: Mirko Ilic Corp.
LOCATION: New York, NY

4
Microsoft Sweden
INDUSTRY: Technology
AGENCY: We Recommend
LOCATION: Copenhagen,
Denmark

Qasim

1

2

3

4

1
Qasim
INDUSTRY: Project Management
AGENCY: Q
LOCATION: Wiesbaden,
Germany

2
O&DS
INDUSTRY: Software
Development
AGENCY: Designaside
LOCATION: Italy

3
Slaant
INDUSTRY: Software
AGENCY: Ian Lynam Creative
Direction & Graphic Design
LOCATION: Tokyo, Japan

4
Bonita
INDUSTRY: Vitamins
AGENCY: Richard Baird Ltd.
LOCATION: Nottingham, UK

inews

1

2

3

BuzzBee

4

1	2	3	4
Office and Data Systems	**Babybites**	**AW Marketing / Dee Patel**	**BuzzBee B2B Marketing**
INDUSTRY: Software Development	INDUSTRY: Social Networking	INDUSTRY: Property Letting	INDUSTRY: Marketing
AGENCY: Designaside	AGENCY: Rizco Designs	AGENCY: Imagine	AGENCY: Mary Hutchison Design LLC
LOCATION: Italy	LOCATION: Manasquan, NJ	LOCATION: Manchester, UK	LOCATION: Seattle, WA

1

2

3

4

1
Butt Thornton & Baehr PC
INDUSTRY: Law
AGENCY: 3 Advertising
LOCATION: Albuquerque, NM

2
SAC Wireless
INDUSTRY: Wireless
Communications Provider
AGENCY: Rule29
LOCATION: Geneva, IL

3
Gamers Insight Group
INDUSTRY: Video Games
Research
AGENCY: Mazziotti Design
LOCATION: Saratoga Springs, UT

4
Jacob Cass
INDUSTRY: Design
AGENCY: Just Creative Design
LOCATION: Cardiff, Australia

Cafe Perk

INDUSTRY: Food & Beverages
AGENCY: Cubiqdesign
LOCATION: Newmarket,
Suffolk, UK

1

2

Frank & Proper®

3

4

1
Smile Africa
INDUSTRY: Non-Profit
AGENCY: Splash:Design
LOCATION: Kelowna, BC,
Canada

2
Pratt Institute
INDUSTRY: Magazine
AGENCY: Reebok International
LOCATION: Boston, MA

3
Self Promotion
INDUSTRY: Advertising &
Design Agency
AGENCY: Frank & Proper
LOCATION: Texas

4
Pratt Institute
INDUSTRY: Food Utensils
AGENCY: Reebok International
LOCATION: Boston, MA

1

2

3

1
Scheyer/SF
INDUSTRY: Music Events
AGENCY: MINE™
LOCATION: San Francisco, CA

2
Ape Texas
INDUSTRY: Non-Profit
AGENCY: D&Dre Creative
LOCATION: Round Rock, TX

3
Cunning Design
INDUSTRY: Design
AGENCY: James Marsh Design
LOCATION: Kent, UK

macrodeck

1

2

3

HOPSCOTCH

HOPSCOTCH*STUDIO*

4

1
Marcodeck
INDUSTRY: Social Networking
AGENCY: Entz Creative
LOCATION: Singapore

2
Pastiche
INDUSTRY: Fashion Boutique
AGENCY: Imagine
LOCATION: Manchester, UK

3
Carneseca Magazine
INDUSTRY: Literature / Art
AGENCY: 288
LOCATION: Rio de Janeiro, Brazil

4
Self-Promotion
INDUSTRY: Design
AGENCY: Hopscotch Studio
LOCATION: Harrisonburg, VA

1

2

3

4

1	2	3	4
Mercury Heating & Cooling	**Radiant**	**Hill Construction Co.**	**Dandelion Products**
INDUSTRY: HVAC Services	INDUSTRY: Communications	INDUSTRY: Construction Co.	INDUSTRY: Consumer Products
AGENCY: D&Dre Creative	AGENCY: D&Dre Creative	AGENCY: Breedlove Creative	AGENCY: Matli Group
LOCATION: Round Rock, TX	LOCATION: Round Rock, TX	LOCATION: San Diego, CA	LOCATION: Los Angeles, CA

FESTIVAL- OG ARRANGEMENTSKONTORET

1

2

SINCE 1955

3

04
DESIGN

4

1
FARK
INDUSTRY: Festival
Arrangement Office
AGENCY: UREDD
LOCATION: Trondheim, Norway

2
Self-Promotion
INDUSTRY: Design
AGENCY: Felt Design Group
LOCATION: Costa Mesa, CA

3
**American Hungarian
Foundation**
INDUSTRY: Non-Profit
AGENCY: Hames Design
LOCATION: Mohegan Lake, NY

4
Ruadesign
INDUSTRY: Design
AGENCY: diografic
LOCATION: Lisbon, Portugal

1

2

3

4

1
Mode
INDUSTRY: Restaurant
AGENCY: Yyes
LOCATION: Minneapolis, MN

2
IenFest
INDUSTRY: Investments
AGENCY: D4 Creative Group
LOCATION: Philadelphia, PA

3
Case Consulting & Projects
INDUSTRY: Consulting
AGENCY: Paraleloz
LOCATION: Maringñi, Parañi,
Brazil

4
Metro Computerworks
INDUSTRY: Computers
AGENCY: Oakley Design
Studios
LOCATION: Portland, OR

Olomomo Nut Co.
INDUSTRY: Food
AGENCY: Moxie Sozo
LOCATION: Boulder, CO

1

gc
good co.

2

M·M TITLE CO.

3

D&
DRE

4

1
Pratt Institute
INDUSTRY: Performing Arts
AGENCY: Reebok International
LOCATION: Boston, MA

2
Good Company Coffee
INDUSTRY: Coffee Shop
AGENCY: Landor Associates
LOCATION: Paris, France

3
M+M Title Co.
INDUSTRY: Title Company
AGENCY: Graphic Impact
LOCATION: Kettering, OH

4
Self-Promotion
INDUSTRY: Design
AGENCY: D&Dre Creative
LOCATION: Round Rock, TX

D•omaining

1

inspire commerce

2

3

architectura plus

4

1

Domaining.com
INDUSTRY: Website
AGENCY: Entz Creative
LOCATION: Singapore

2

Inspire Commerce
INDUSTRY: E-Commerce
AGENCY: Moxie Sozo
LOCATION: Boulder, CO

3

MD
INDUSTRY: Marketing
AGENCY: Bogdan Terente
LOCATION: Iasi, Romania

4

Architectural Plus
INDUSTRY: Architecture
AGENCY: Storm Corporate Design
LOCATION: Auckland, New Zealand

1
Shore Scores
INDUSTRY: Music Studio
AGENCY: D4 Creative Group
LOCATION: Philadelphia, PA

2
Southstar Shipping Limited
INDUSTRY: Transportation
AGENCY: Entz Creative
LOCATION: Singapore

numb

1

2

MARTIAN
RANCH & VINEYARD

3

JOHN MILLHAUSER
ART DIRECTION

4

1
Numb Popsicle Stands
INDUSTRY: Popsicle Retailer
AGENCY: D&Dre Creative
LOCATION: Round Rock, TX

2
Land & Sky
INDUSTRY: Luxury
Accommodation
AGENCY: Agitprop Design &
Communications
LOCATION: London, UK

3
Martian Ranch & Vineyard
INDUSTRY: Winemaker
AGENCY: Geyrhalter Design
LOCATION: Santa Monica, CA

4
**John Millhauser Art
Direction**
INDUSTRY: Photography
AGENCY: Ian Lynam Creative
Direction & Graphic Design
LOCATION: Tokyo, Japan

SCISSOR WERKS

1

PARK TAHOE
—————— INN ——————

2

Association for
TRUE HOSPITALITY

3

THE SWEETESTLAND
A NEW DOCUMENTARY FILM

4

1
Scissor Werks
INDUSTRY: Knife Sharpening
AGENCY: UNIT Design
Collective
LOCATION: San Francisco, CA

2
Park Tahoe Inn
INDUSTRY: Hospitality
AGENCY: Geyrhalter Design
LOCATION: Santa Monica, CA

3
Association for
True Hospitality
INDUSTRY: Hospitality
AGENCY: Bronson Ma Creative
LOCATION: San Antonio, TX

4
The Sweetest Land
INDUSTRY: Entertainment
AGENCY: NP Graphic Design
LOCATION: Simsbury, CT

1

2

3

1
Columbus Museum
INDUSTRY: Columbus Museum
AGENCY: Andy Gabbert Design
LOCATION: Oakland, CA

2
Cornerstone
INDUSTRY: Non-Profit
AGENCY: Maycreate Idea
Group
LOCATION: Chattanooga, TN

3
Tanzore
INDUSTRY: Restaurant/Bar/
Lounge
AGENCY: AkarStudios
LOCATION: Santa Monica, CA

1

2

3

1
MDM
INDUSTRY: Furniture
AGENCY: YESDESIGNGROUP
LOCATION: Los Angeles, CA

2
Dish
INDUSTRY: Restaurant
AGENCY: Riley Designs
LOCATION: Basalt, CO

3
Arts Engagement Exchange
INDUSTRY: Arts
AGENCY: Entz Creative
LOCATION: Singapore

1

2

3

4

1	2	3	4
Veson Nautical	**Upplevelseindustrin**	**Scientific Notation**	**Grand View Development**
INDUSTRY: Maritime	INDUSTRY: Creative Industries	INDUSTRY: Copywriting	INDUSTRY: Real-Estate
AGENCY: Marquis Design	AGENCY: We Recommend	AGENCY: Creative Squall	AGENCY: Kolano Design
LOCATION: Boston, MA	LOCATION: Copenhagen, Denmark	LOCATION: Trophy Club, TX	LOCATION: Pittsburgh, PA

The Thread Room

INDUSTRY: Yarn & Textile
Retailer

AGENCY: housemouse

LOCATION: Melbourne,
Australia

1

2

3

4

1
Media Everywhere
INDUSTRY: Satellite Uplink
AGENCY: D4 Creative Group
LOCATION: Philadelphia, PA

2
Self-Promotion
INDUSTRY: Marketing
AGENCY: Say Agency
LOCATION: Buenos Aires,
Argentina

3
Self-Promotion
INDUSTRY: Advertising Agency
AGENCY: D4 Creative Group
LOCATION: Philadelphia, PA

4
Think AV
INDUSTRY: Audio I Visual
AGENCY: Oakley Design
LOCATION: Portland, OR

1

TimeWhale

2

econic events

3

1
**Southern Hills Baptist
Church**
INDUSTRY: Religion
AGENCY: Matcha Design
LOCATION: Tulsa, OK

2
TimeWhale.com
INDUSTRY: Software
AGENCY: Geyrhalter Design
LOCATION: Santa Monica, CA

3
Econic Events
INDUSTRY: Event Planning
AGENCY: twolineSTUDIO
LOCATION: Denver, CO

Terapia em Foco
Psicólogos associados
INDUSTRY: Health
AGENCY: 288
LOCATION: Rio de Janeiro,
Brazil

1

2

3

4

1
Elé Cake Company
INDUSTRY: Dessert Retailer
AGENCY: Pryor Design Company
LOCATION: Ann Arbor, MI

2
Sandy Leong
INDUSTRY: Jewelry
AGENCY: The O Group
LOCATION: New York, NY

3
**The Wright Real
Estate Company**
INDUSTRY: Real Estate
AGENCY: Thinkhaus
LOCATION: Richmond, VA

4
Blomsterbixen
INDUSTRY: Retail
AGENCY: We Recommend
LOCATION: Copenhagen,
Denmark

MOVING   IMAGES

1

IN**FOREST**
communications

2

10 26
TEN26 DESIGN GROUP

3

4

1
Media Mötesplats Malmö
INDUSTRY: Conference
AGENCY: We Recommend
LOCATION: Copenhagen,
Denmark

2
Inforest Communications
INDUSTRY: Communications
AGENCY: KO11 Design
LOCATION: East Brunswick, NJ

3
Self-Promotion
INDUSTRY: Design
AGENCY: Ten26 Design
Group, Inc.
LOCATION: Crystal Lake, IL

4
Longworth Industries
INDUSTRY: Apparel
AGENCY: Airtype Studio
LOCATION: Winston-Salem, NC

Villaggio
— · *h o m e s* · —

1

2

3

ra i nswear

4

1
Villaggio Homes
INDUSTRY: Real Estate
AGENCY: Bronson Ma Creative
LOCATION: San Antonio, TX

2
Fria Light Ice Cream
INDUSTRY: Ice Cream Retailer
AGENCY: Pryor Design
Company
LOCATION: Ann Arbor, MI

3
Covia Realty
INDUSTRY: Real Estate
AGENCY: Bronson Ma Creative
LOCATION: San Antonio, TX

4
Rainswear
INDUSTRY: Fashion
AGENCY: Bronson Ma Creative
LOCATION: San Antonio, TX

1

2

Taproot
INDUSTRY: Music
AGENCY: Ian Lynam Creative
Direction & Graphic Design
LOCATION: Tokyo , Japan

2

Darlings of the day
INDUSTRY: Music
AGENCY: Biz-R
LOCATION: Totnes, UK

1

LEND A HAND

2

1
AIGA Los Angeles
INDUSTRY: Design
AGENCY: UNIT Design
Collective
LOCATION: San Francisco, CA

2
**Tyler School of Art Graphic
& Interactive Design
Department**
INDUSTRY: Design
AGENCY: Calagraphic Design
LOCATION: Elkins Park, PA

1

Hot Milk
INDUSTRY: Design
AGENCY: zerokw
LOCATION: Marche, Pesaro,
Italy

2

The Intech Group
INDUSTRY: Telecommunications
AGENCY: Airtype Studio
LOCATION: Winston-Salem, MA

3

West Chester Township
INDUSTRY: Government
AGENCY: Five Visual
Communication & Design
LOCATION: Mason, OH

1

2

Liquid Assets Global / Diageo
INDUSTRY: Hospitality
AGENCY: Tangent Graphic
LOCATION: Glasgow,
Lanarkshire, UK

Prima Cinema™
INDUSTRY: Home Entertainment
AGENCY: The UXB
LOCATION: Beverly Hills, CA

1

2

ooh l♥vely!

3

1
Boynk
INDUSTRY: Sports
AGENCY: D4 Creative Group
LOCATION: Philadelphia, PA

2
Voce Romantica
INDUSTRY: Performing Arts
AGENCY: Design Nut, LLC
LOCATION: Kensington, MD

3
Ooh Lovely! Invitations
INDUSTRY: Greeting Cards
AGENCY: Laughing Lion Design
LOCATION: Westmeath, AL

1

2

3

1	2	3
Gym Concepts LLC	**Lumeta®**	**ID Diagnostics**
INDUSTRY: Fitness	INDUSTRY: Solar Power	INDUSTRY: Medical
AGENCY: Legacy Design Group	AGENCY: The UXB	AGENCY: Stressdesign
LOCATION: Hockley, TX	LOCATION: Beverly Hills, CA	LOCATION: Syracuse, NY

1

2

3

1
Zumiez
INDUSTRY: Action Sports
Apparel
AGENCY: Weather Control
LOCATION: Seattle, WA

2
Bell Mountain Massage
INDUSTRY: Health & Wellness
AGENCY: Handcrafted Media
LOCATION: Monument, CO

3
School's Out Washington
INDUSTRY: Education
AGENCY: Weather Control
LOCATION: Seattle, WA

1

2

1
ReMax Midway
INDUSTRY: Real Estate
AGENCY: Thinkhaus
LOCATION: Richmond, VA

2
Starr Tincup
INDUSTRY: Marketing
AGENCY: Creative Squall
LOCATION: Trophy Club, TX

Qwest Field
INDUSTRY: Sports
AGENCY: Levy Restaurants
LOCATION: Chicago, IL

1

2

3

4

1
**Universidad Autonoma
de Guadalajara**
INDUSTRY: Education
AGENCY: Kenneth Diseño
LOCATION: Uruapan,
Michoacan, Mexico

2
Self-Promotion
INDUSTRY: Design
AGENCY: Odigy Studio
LOCATION: Brunei Darussalam

3
Tenet Group
INDUSTRY: Non-Profit Telecom
AGENCY: UNIT Design
Collective
LOCATION: San Francisco, CA

4
Brian + Co.
INDUSTRY: Real Estate
AGENCY: House of Tears Design
LOCATION: Kansas City, MO

COMBINATION
MARKS

1

2

3

4

1
Badcock Vodka
INDUSTRY: Spirits
AGENCY: Scott Creative
LOCATION: Omaha, NE

2
Seraphoenix
INDUSTRY: Art
AGENCY: XYARTS
LOCATION: Braeside, Victoria,
Australia

3
Merak
INDUSTRY: Logistic Business
AGENCY: Alterego
LOCATION: Merida, Mexico

4
Cachiq
INDUSTRY: Fashion
AGENCY: XYARTS
LOCATION: Braeside, Victoria,
Australia

ONE LEGACY GROUP

1

SINGH FAMILY CELLARS

2

1
One Legacy Group
INDUSTRY: Real Estate
AGENCY: Weather Control
LOCATION: Seattle, WA

2
Singh Family Cellars
INDUSTRY: Wine Maker
AGENCY: Mariana Pabon
LOCATION: San Francisco, CA

1

2

3

1
**Schussler Creative /
Orange County Choppers**
INDUSTRY: Hospitality
AGENCY: Levy Restaurants
LOCATION: Chicago, IL

2
Self-Promotion
INDUSTRY: Interactive
AGENCY: Automatic Partners,
LLC
LOCATION: Irvine, CA

3
Snowjoe
INDUSTRY: Retail
AGENCY: Rubin Design
LOCATION: Staten Island, NY

1

2

3

1
TSC
INDUSTRY: Software
AGENCY: AxiomaCero
LOCATION: Monterrey,
Nuevo Leon, Mexico

2
Self-Promotion
INDUSTRY: Music
AGENCY: AlterEgo
LOCATION: Merida, Mexico

3
East-West Marketing
INDUSTRY: Marketing
AGENCY: Paper Tower
LOCATION: Elgin, IL

1

2

3

4

1
Brooklyn's Bounty
INDUSTRY: Agriculture
AGENCY: Pratt Institute
LOCATION: Whitestone, NY

2
**Too Many Teeth
Productions**
INDUSTRY: Entertainment
AGENCY: SNAUT.com
LOCATION: Los Angeles, CA

3
Brown Cow Pantry
INDUSTRY: Gourmet Food
AGENCY: Miller Creative, LLC
LOCATION: Lakewood, NJ

4
Fresh Cutt
INDUSTRY: Fast Casual Dining
AGENCY: AkarStudios
LOCATION: Santa Monica, CA

1

2

3

4

1
Self-Promotion
INDUSTRY: Design
AGENCY: Ribbons of Red
LOCATION: Cincinnati, OH

2
Likatek
INDUSTRY: Music
AGENCY: projectGRAPHICS.EU
LOCATION: Prishtina, Kosova,
Albania

3
Handsome Cycles
INDUSTRY: Bicycles-Retail
AGENCY: Periscope
LOCATION: Minneapolis, MN

4
Arteis
INDUSTRY: Cigar
AGENCY: GaxDesign
LOCATION: Guadalajara,
Mexico

Dry Fly Distilling
INDUSTRY: Spirits
AGENCY: HL2
LOCATION: Seattle, WA

InSpira
INDUSTRY: Performing Arts
AGENCY: 3rd Edge
Communications
LOCATION: Jersey City, NJ

1

2

3

4

1
Alan Jackson
INDUSTRY: Music
AGENCY: Ian Lynam Creative
Direction & Graphic Design
LOCATION: Tokyo, Japan

2
Frederick Arts Council
INDUSTRY: Arts Organization
AGENCY: Kalico Design
LOCATION: Frederick, MD

3
Regina di Picche
INDUSTRY: Fashion
AGENCY: Synthview
LOCATION: Paris, France

4
Mercatino
INDUSTRY: Food/Restaurant
AGENCY: Maycreate Idea Group
LOCATION: Chattanooga, TN

1

2

3

4

1
Brewha! Brewery
INDUSTRY: Beer Brewing
AGENCY: Whatislight
LOCATION: TN

2
Eddie Bauer
INDUSTRY: Apparel & Outdoor
Gear
AGENCY: Weather Control
LOCATION: Seattle, WA

3
The Upper Room Ministries
INDUSTRY: Non-profit
AGENCY: Anderson Design Group
LOCATION: Nashville, TN

4
Giving Children Hope
INDUSTRY: Non-Profit
AGENCY: Fox Fire Creative
LOCATION: Highlands Ranch,
CO

Flock
INDUSTRY: Fashion Boutique
AGENCY: Alphabet Arm
LOCATION: Boston, MA

1

2

1

Yarraville Arts Festival Inc.
INDUSTRY: Non Profit
AGENCY: housemouse
LOCATION: Melbourne,
Victoria, Australia

2

**European Youth Card
Association**
INDUSTRY: Youth Travel
AGENCY: Niedermeier Design
LOCATION: Seattle, WA

1

2

3

4

1

Valmann
INDUSTRY: Nightlife
AGENCY: Nico Ammann
LOCATION: Zurich, Switzerland

2

Char-Broil
INDUSTRY: Barbecue Products
AGENCY: Andy Gabbert Design
LOCATION: Oakland, CA

3

Uniflux Filters
INDUSTRY: Automotive
AGENCY: Stefan Romanu
LOCATION: Timisoara, Romania

4

National Theatre of Kosova
INDUSTRY: Theatre
AGENCY: projectGRAPHICS.EU
LOCATION: Prishtina, Kosova,
Albania

1

2

3

1
Mapleshade
INDUSTRY: Music
AGENCY: VanPelt Creative
LOCATION: Garland, TX

2
Smokewood
Entertainment Group
INDUSTRY: Entertainment
AGENCY: Moxie Sozo
LOCATION: Boulder, CO

3
Val Spicer
INDUSTRY: Floral Foam
Manufacturer
AGENCY: Biz-R
LOCATION: Totnes, UK

1

2

1

X-Sense Events
INDUSTRY: Music /
Entertainment
AGENCY: John Beckers
LOCATION: Rotterdam,
Netherlands

2

**Portland Documentary &
eXperimental Film Festival**
INDUSTRY: Film
AGENCY: Ian Lynam Creative
Direction & Graphic Design
LOCATION: Tokyo, Japan

1

2

1
Frucor
INDUSTRY: Energy Drinks
AGENCY: The Saltmine
LOCATION: Sydney, Australia

2
Skate the Streets
INDUSTRY: Youth Apparel
AGENCY: UNIT Design
Collective
LOCATION: San Francisco, CA

1

2

3

4

1

Ables Landscaping
INDUSTRY: Landscaping
AGENCY: Open Creative Group
LOCATION: Birmingham, AL

2

**Mission Minded
for Hope SF**
INDUSTRY: Non Profit
AGENCY: Mariana Pabon
LOCATION: San Francisco, CA

3

**Alabama Museums
Association**
INDUSTRY: Professional
Association
AGENCY: Open Creative Group
LOCATION: Birmingham, AL

4

Arteis
INDUSTRY: Food & Beverages
AGENCY: GaxDesign
LOCATION: Guadalajara,
Mexico

1

2

1
Macadamia Natural Oil
INDUSTRY: Haircare
AGENCY: Version-X Design
Corp.
LOCATION: Burbank, CA

2
Saturday Gourmet
INDUSTRY: Catering /
Restaurant
AGENCY: Open Creative Group
LOCATION: Birmingham, AL

Brian Olsen - Art In Action
INDUSTRY: Entertainment
AGENCY: BrandSavvy, Inc.
LOCATION: Highlands Ranch, CO

1

2

SPORTZ DAWGZ

3

healthy**spot.**

4

1	2	3	4
Sound Foundation, LLC	**New York Racing Association**	**Sound Foundation, LLC**	**Healthy Spot**
INDUSTRY: Education	INDUSTRY: Sports	INDUSTRY: Dog Toys	INDUSTRY: Dog - Retail / Daycare / Spa
AGENCY: UNIT Design Collective	AGENCY: Mike Carsten	AGENCY: UNIT Design Collective	AGENCY: AkarStudios
LOCATION: San Francisco, CA	LOCATION: Middle Village, NY	LOCATION: San Francisco, CA	LOCATION: Santa Monica, CA

EAIGEN AGRITECH

1

ENCLAVE RISING

2

The Ultimate
IT Community

3

4

1
Eaigen Agritech Ltd.
INDUSTRY: Agriculture Lab
AGENCY: Storm Corporate
Design
LOCATION: Auckland,
New Zealand

2
Enclave Rising
INDUSTRY: Real Estate
AGENCY: Alphabet Arm
LOCATION: Boston, MA

3
Center For IT Leadership
INDUSTRY: Professional /
Social Networking Site
AGENCY: Coloryn Studio
LOCATION: Richmond, VA

4
Moustache Sally
INDUSTRY: Humor Website
& Blog
AGENCY: Alphabet Arm
LOCATION: Boston, MA

1

2

1

Birchtree Photography
INDUSTRY: Photography
AGENCY: DavidPCrawford.com
LOCATION: Pittsburgh, PA

2

I Love Your Dress
INDUSTRY: Online Retail
AGENCY: Clockwork Studios
LOCATION: San Antonio, TX

1

2

Women's Business Lunch

3

4

1

Fatty Gets A Stylist
INDUSTRY: Music
AGENCY: Alphabet Arm
LOCATION: Boston, MA

2

Pink Rhino Kids
INDUSTRY: Children's Apparel
AGENCY: Komprehensive
Design
LOCATION: King of Prussia, PA

3

Women's Business Lunch
INDUSTRY: Networking
AGENCY: Wibye Advertising
& Graphic Design
LOCATION: London, UK

4

Sweet Annie's Catering
INDUSTRY: Catering
AGENCY: Mediaworks
LOCATION: Bloomington, IN

1

2

3

4

1
Scrapallier
INDUSTRY: Scrapbook
AGENCY: Matcha Design
LOCATION: Tulsa, OK

2
Self-Promotion
INDUSTRY: Design
AGENCY: JohnBoerckel.com
LOCATION: Havertown, PA

3
Cubiqdesign Limited
INDUSTRY: Graphic Design
AGENCY: Cubiqdesign
LOCATION: Newmarket,
Suffolk, UK

4
Maripepas
INDUSTRY: Sports
AGENCY: Kenneth Diseã'o
LOCATION: Uruapan,
Michoacan, Mexico

CRESCENT DRIVE
ENTERTAINMENT

1

2

ELLIS BROS.
messengers

3

THE BULL & WHISTLE
PUB & EATERY

4

1
Rock 'n' Roll Camp for Girls
INDUSTRY: Education
AGENCY: Plazm
LOCATION: Portland, OR

2
**Crescent Drive
Entertainment**
INDUSTRY: Entertainment
AGENCY: YYES
LOCATION: Minneapolis, MN

3
Ellis Brothers Messengers
INDUSTRY: Bike Messengers
AGENCY: Oakley Design
Studios
LOCATION: Portland, OR

4
The Bull and Whistle
INDUSTRY: Restaurant/Bar
AGENCY: Symbiotic Solutions
LOCATION: Lansing, MI

1

2

3

4

1
Piedmont Distillers
INDUSTRY: Consumer Goods
AGENCY: Airtype Studio
LOCATION: Winston-Salem, NC

2
American University Depart-
ment of Performing Arts
INDUSTRY: Education
AGENCY: Chemi Montes
Design
LOCATION: Falls Church, VA

3
Eddie Bauer
INDUSTRY: Outdoor Apparel
AGENCY: Weather Control
LOCATION: Seattle, WA

3
Outlaw Tattoo
INDUSTRY: Tattoo Parlor
AGENCY: Breedlove Creative
LOCATION: San Diego, CA

1

2

Give Something Back
International

3

ACTION NOW!

4

1
Autism Community Network
INDUSTRY: Non Profit
AGENCY: Clockwork Studios
LOCATION: San Antonio, TX

2
Victorian Safe Communities Network Inc.
INDUSTRY: Non-Profit
AGENCY: housemouse
LOCATION: Melbourne, Victoria, Australia

3
Give Something Back International
INDUSTRY: Non-Profit
AGENCY: Gee + Chung Design
LOCATION: San Francisco, CA

4
Action Now Network
INDUSTRY: Volunteer Organization
AGENCY: Siah Design
LOCATION: Alberta, Canada

West Penn **Energy Solutions**

1

2

3

1
West Penn Energy Solutions
INDUSTRY: Energy
AGENCY: Imagebox
Productions Inc.
LOCATION: Pittsburgh, PA

2
International Floral Service
INDUSTRY: Flower Designer
AGENCY: Zerokw
LOCATION: Pesaro, Italy

3
Tee
INDUSTRY: CRM Software
AGENCY: Siah Design
LOCATION: Alberta, Canada

Melrose Dog Society
INDUSTRY: Community
Pet Organization
AGENCY: Alphabet Arm
LOCATION: Boston, MA

Finnegans Irish Amber
INDUSTRY: Non-Profit Beer
Company
AGENCY: Periscope
LOCATION: Minneapolis, MN

1

2

3

4

1
Pigtale Books
INDUSTRY: Publishing
AGENCY: Coloryn Studio
LOCATION: Richmond, VA

2
Resort Suites
INDUSTRY: Hospitality
AGENCY: Z2 Marketing +
Design
LOCATION: Pewaukee, WI

3
Chameleon Copy
INDUSTRY: Copywriter
AGENCY: YIU Studio
LOCATION: Seattle, WA

4
**Green Earth Corporate
Kindness Organization**
INDUSTRY: Corporate
Consultant
AGENCY: Roskelly Inc.
LOCATION: Portsmouth, RI

curiousfish

1

2

3

1
Curious Fish Marketing
INDUSTRY: Marketing
AGENCY: D&Dre Creative
LOCATION: Round Rock, TX

2
Butterfly Effect
INDUSTRY: Recording Artist
AGENCY: AmericanDesign-Co.com
LOCATION: Los Angeles, CA

3
Life In Abundance International
INDUSTRY: Non-Profit
AGENCY: Rule29
LOCATION: Geneva, IL

Jordan Brookes
INDUSTRY: Leisure / Fitness
AGENCY: Imagine
LOCATION: Manchester, UK

1

2

1
Camel City Cruisers
Scooter Club
INDUSTRY: Recreation
AGENCY: Fifth Letter
LOCATION: Winston-Salem, NC

2
Arteis
INDUSTRY: Restaurant / Food
AGENCY: GaxDesign
LOCATION: Guadalajara,
Mexico

DIRTY
PICTURES, INC.

1

MacDonald
PHOTOGRAPHY

2

3

4

1
Dirty Pictures
INDUSTRY: Entertainment
AGENCY: YYES
LOCATION: Minneapolis, MN

2
MacDonald Photography
INDUSTRY: Photography
AGENCY: Rule29
LOCATION: Geneva, IL

3
Mark Gooch
INDUSTRY: Photography
AGENCY: DogStar Design
LOCATION: Birmingham, AL

4
Limber Vilorio
INDUSTRY: Comtemporary Art
AGENCY: Fernando Rodriguez, Inc.
LOCATION: Santo Domminigo, Dominican Republic

1

2

3

1
Marc Preston Productions
INDUSTRY: Entertainment
AGENCY: Odigy
LOCATION: Brunei Darussalam

2
**Pixelclub Interactive
Media Agency**
INDUSTRY: Design
AGENCY: Odigy
LOCATION: Brunei Darussalam

3
Self-Promotion
INDUSTRY: Communication
AGENCY: NalinDesign
LOCATION: Neuenrade,
Germany

1

2

3

4

1
GoLite
INDUSTRY: Outdoor Gear
& Apparel
AGENCY: Moxie Sozo
LOCATION: Boulder, CO

2
Lovesh Sharma
INDUSTRY: Web Development
AGENCY: Odigy
LOCATION: Brunei Darussalam

3
H&M Racing
INDUSTRY: Youth Group
AGENCY: Creative Squall
LOCATION: Trophy Club, TX

4
Daniele Volpini
INDUSTRY: Nautic
AGENCY: Zerokw
LOCATION: Pesaro, Italy

1

2

3

4

1
The Cult
INDUSTRY: Music
AGENCY: Ian Lynam Creative
Direction & Graphic Design
LOCATION: Tokyo, Japan

2
Keigan Boarding Apparel
INDUSTRY: Fashion
AGENCY: Entz Creative
LOCATION: Singapore

3
Dore
INDUSTRY: Automotive
AGENCY: Zerokw
LOCATION: Pesaro, Italy

4
**Tidy Tom's Cleaning
Company**
INDUSTRY: Residential Service
AGENCY: ohTwentyone
LOCATION: Colleyville, TX

A-KOM

INDUSTRY: Corporate
Communication
AGENCY: Graphic Design
Studio by Yurko Gutsulyak
LOCATION: Kyiv, Ukraine

1

2

3

1

Le Pigeon

INDUSTRY: Restaurant

AGENCY: Ian Lynam Creative

Direction & Graphic Design

LOCATION: Tokyo, Japan

2

LionStone

INDUSTRY: Real Estate

AGENCY: Kaimere

LOCATION: Dubai,

United Arab Emirates

3

Loop. A place for

videoart lovers

INDUSTRY: Videoart

AGENCY: Fran Rosa Soler

LOCATION: Spain

1

2

3

1
Fisiogim
INDUSTRY: Physiotherapy
Centre
AGENCY: 2creativo
LOCATION: Barcelona, Spain

2
Crystal Clear Bags Canada
INDUSTRY: Supplier of
Plastic Bags for Retailers
AGENCY: Niedermeier Design
LOCATION: Seattle, WA

3
ONRAX
INDUSTRY: Garage Storage /
Makeovers
AGENCY: Niedermeier Design
LOCATION: Seattle, WA

1

2

3

4

1	2	3	4
RediStat	**Haselden Construction**	**Red Jacket Resorts**	**TRG**
INDUSTRY: Health Care	INDUSTRY: Construction	INDUSTRY: Hospitality	INDUSTRY: Customer Solutions
AGENCY: Sandals Resorts	AGENCY: BrandSavvy, Inc.	AGENCY: Roskelly Inc.	AGENCY: D4 Creative Group
LOCATION: Miami, FL	LOCATION: Highlands Ranch, CO	LOCATION: Portsmouth, RI	LOCATION: Philadelphia, PA

1

2

3

4

1
**University of California,
Los Angeles**
INDUSTRY: Education
AGENCY: Ramp Creative+
Design
LOCATION: Los Angeles, CA

2
Childhood Stroke Network
INDUSTRY: Non-Profit
AGENCY: Clockwork Studios
LOCATION: San Antonio, TX

3
Sweet Sweets
INDUSTRY: Candy, Retail Shop
AGENCY: Doug Barrett Design
LOCATION: Birmingham, AL

4
Grace Church
INDUSTRY: Religion
AGENCY: Holy Cow Creative
LOCATION: Midland, MI

1

Vinska Druzba Slovenije
INDUSTRY: Wine Union
Of Slovenia
AGENCY: Krog
LOCATION: Ljubljana, Slovenia

2

Parago
INDUSTRY: Technology
AGENCY: Bronson Ma Creative
LOCATION: San Antonio, TX

3

Scoopal
INDUSTRY: Data Gathering
AGENCY: Niedermeier Design
LOCATION: Seattle, WA

4

**NORD National Organization
for Rare Diseases**
INDUSTRY: Non-Profit
AGENCY: SandorMax
LOCATION: Sandy Hook, CT

1

2

3

4

1
Bytware
INDUSTRY: Technology
AGENCY: Stellar Debris
LOCATION: Hadano,
Kanagawa, Japan

2
Yak Academy
INDUSTRY: Education
AGENCY: Flux Business
Communications
LOCATION: Culver City, CA

3
Ripple Water Campaign
INDUSTRY: Environmental
AGENCY: Little Jacket
LOCATION: Cleveland, OH

4
KolorID
INDUSTRY: Color Identification
Products
AGENCY: Tyler Sticka, Interac-
tive Design & Illustration
LOCATION: Portland, OR

1

2

3

4

1

Tier Logic, Inc.
INDUSTRY: Semi Conductors
AGENCY: Marc Posch
Design, Inc.
LOCATION: Long Beach, CA

2

NEXCESS Hosting Solutions
INDUSTRY: Internet Hosting
AGENCY: Pryor Design Company
LOCATION: Ann Arbor, MI

3

ULitho Print Services
INDUSTRY: Printing Services
AGENCY: Pryor Design Company
LOCATION: Ann Arbor, MI

4

Soundsgood Paris
INDUSTRY: Music
AGENCY: Subcommunication
LOCATION: Montreal, QC,
Canada

GENERATION
FINANCIAL SERVICES LTD

1

INSTITUTO KANNON

2

KAMALA FILMS

3

ACANTHUS
DEVELOPMENT GROUP

4

1
Generation Financial Services
INDUSTRY: Finance
AGENCY: Cubiqdesign
LOCATION: Newmarket, Suffolk, UK

2
Kannon Intitute
INDUSTRY: Health
AGENCY: Alterego
LOCATION: Merida, Mexico

3
Kamala Films
INDUSTRY: Entertainment
AGENCY: Rizco Design
LOCATION: Manasquan, NJ

4
Acanthus Development Group
INDUSTRY: Real Estate
AGENCY: Breedlove Creative
LOCATION: San Diego, CA

1

2

3

4

1
Eco Trade
INDUSTRY: Heavy Industry
AGENCY: projectGRAPHICS.EU
LOCATION: Prishtina, Kosova,
Albania

2
Tapuz International Trading
INDUSTRY: Wholesale
AGENCY: Orange Bike Design
LOCATION: Los Angeles, CA

3
Self-Promotion
INDUSTRY: Design
AGENCY: Creative Squall
LOCATION: Trophy Club, TX

4
**Greater New York Health
Association**
INDUSTRY: Health Care
AGENCY: Langton Cherubino
Group
LOCATION: New York, NY

Wholesome Photography
INDUSTRY: Photography
AGENCY: Wholesome Design
LOCATION: Birmingham, AL

1

2

3

4

1
Oceania
INDUSTRY: Health & Beauty
AGENCY: XYARTS
LOCATION: Braeside, Victoria,
Australia

2
**Aquanaut Capital
Management**
INDUSTRY: Financial
AGENCY: Remo Strada Design
LOCATION: Lincroft, NJ

3
Seaside Satellite
INDUSTRY: Communications
Company
AGENCY: D&Dre Creative
LOCATION: Round Rock, TX

4
True Nicks
INDUSTRY: Horse Racing
AGENCY: Roskelly Inc.
LOCATION: Portsmouth, RI

BiblioFile

carbonpeople

1
Edgewise Concrete
INDUSTRY: Construction
AGENCY: Imagebox
Productions, Inc.
LOCATION: Pittsburgh, PA

2
Next Step
INDUSTRY: Human Resources
AGENCY: William Salit Design
LOCATION: San Francisco, CA

3
Biblio File
INDUSTRY: Online software
AGENCY: Ocular Ink
LOCATION: Nashville, TN

4
Carbon People
INDUSTRY: Sustainable Building
AGENCY: Studio ThreefiftySeven
LOCATION: Adelaide, Australia

B R I D G E **P O I N T** C R E A T I V E

1

THEGAMEWORLD

2

synexis|cg

3

SOUTHERN PINES
CHIROPRACTIC CENTER

4

1
Bridgepoint Creative
INDUSTRY: Strategic
Communications
AGENCY: Avive
LOCATION: Portland, OR

2
The Game World
INDUSTRY: Entertainment
AGENCY: Entz Creative
LOCATION: Singapore

3
Synexis cg
INDUSTRY: Public Relations
AGENCY: Wing Chan
Design, Inc.
LOCATION: New York, NY

4
**Southern Pines
Chiropractic Center**
INDUSTRY: Chiropractor
AGENCY: Open Creative Group
LOCATION: Birmingham, AL

1

2

3

4

1	2	3	4
Chuck the Yuck	**Aussie Rob Foundation**	**Savvy Girls of Summer**	**Arteis**
INDUSTRY: Consumer products	INDUSTRY: Welfare	INDUSTRY: book authors	INDUSTRY: Pet Foods
AGENCY: Avive	AGENCY: Entz Creative	AGENCY: Defteling Design	AGENCY: GaxDesign
LOCATION: Portland, OR	LOCATION: Singapore	LOCATION: Portland, OR	LOCATION: Guadalajara, Mexico

Lisa Rigby Photography
INDUSTRY: Photography
AGENCY: Alphabet Arm
LOCATION: Boston, MA

1

2

3

4

1
Tarrant Pacific
INDUSTRY: Construction
AGENCY: Niedermeier Design
LOCATION: Seattle, WA

2
Infoca
INDUSTRY: Information
Communication
AGENCY: Entz Creative
LOCATION: Singapore

3
Boathouse Living
INDUSTRY: Boating
AGENCY: Thinkhaus
LOCATION: Richmond, VA

4
Keenpixel
INDUSTRY: Graphic Design
AGENCY: Ocular Ink
LOCATION: Nashville, TN

1

2

3

1
Pure Detail
INDUSTRY: Mobile Auto Detailing
AGENCY: The Greater
Good Design
LOCATION: Saint Cloud, FL

2
TwoIn
INDUSTRY: Engineering
Projects of Digital Home &
Sustainability
AGENCY: 2creativo
LOCATION: Barcelona, Spain

3
BlueLake Ventures
INDUSTRY: Financial
AGENCY: Talbot Design
Group, Inc.
LOCATION: Westlake Village, CA

1

HIGHLY
RELEVANT

2

3

4

1
**Association of Legal
Administrators**
INDUSTRY: Membership
Organization
AGENCY: BrandSavvy, Inc.
LOCATION: Highlands Ranch, CO

2
Highly Relevant
INDUSTRY: Digital Marketing
AGENCY: Koren Nelson Design
LOCATION: Los Angeles, CA

3
VoteLink
INDUSTRY: Internet Community
AGENCY: Moxie Sozo
LOCATION: Boulder, CO

4
Self-Promotion
INDUSTRY: Design
AGENCY: Camp Creative Group
LOCATION: Blue Ridge
Summit, PA

1

2

3

1
Kahani World
INDUSTRY: Videos for Kids
AGENCY: Kosta Mijic
LOCATION: Serbia

2
Self-Promotion
INDUSTRY: Branding
Design Studio
AGENCY: YIU Studio
LOCATION: Seattle, WA

3
Lead Like Jesus
INDUSTRY: Religion
AGENCY: Rule29
LOCATION: Geneva, IL

1

2

Autry West Fest
INDUSTRY: Regional Event
AGENCY: B.G. Design
LOCATION: Los Angeles, CA

2

Delrosa International, Inc
INDUSTRY: Custom Construction
AGENCY: Oakley Design Studios
LOCATION: Portland, OR

1

2

CONSUMMATE PET

Your pet. Our passion.

3

1
Dyana Valentine
INDUSTRY: Life Coach
AGENCY: RDQLUS Creative
LOCATION: Omaha, NE

2
Bleu Sur Bleu
AGENCY: Hair Salon
INDUSTRY: Mazziotti Design
LOCATION: Saratoga Springs, UT

3
Consummate Pet
INDUSTRY: Pet Care
AGENCY: The Greater
Good Design
LOCATION: Saint Cloud, FL

jacobus

1

SUNSET VINE
TOWER

2

THE RIDGES
PARIS MOUNTAIN

3

1
Jacobus Consulting
INDUSTRY: Consulting
AGENCY: Marc Posch
Design, Inc.
LOCATION: Los Angeles, CA

2
CIM Group
INDUSTRY: Real-Estate
AGENCY: Ramp
Creative+Design
LOCATION: Los Angeles, CA

3
**The Ridges at
Paris Mountain**
INDUSTRY: Real-Estate
AGENCY: Breedlove Creative
LOCATION: San Diego, CA

SUDACHI

1

greenlivingconsulting

2

GREENSTREET

3

renú

a hair salon

4

1
The Designtist Group
INDUSTRY: Food / Restaurant
AGENCY: Koren Nelson Design
LOCATION: Los Angeles, CA

2
Green Living Consulting
INDUSTRY: Consultants
AGENCY: Ripe.com
LOCATION: Washington, DC

3
Green Street
INDUSTRY: Real Estate
AGENCY: Maycreate
Idea Group
LOCATION: Chattanooga, TN

4
Renú a Hair Salon
INDUSTRY: Hair Salon
AGENCY: Sabrah Maple Design
LOCATION: AL

ACHIEVA HEALTH
Eglinton Bayview Physiotherapy Centre

1

CAUSE CONNECTIONS

2

3

1
Achieva Health inc.
INDUSTRY: Health
AGENCY: Mohographic Inc,
LOCATION: North York, Ontario,
Canada

2
Cause Connections
INDUSTRY: Philanthropy
AGENCY: Sage Systems
LOCATION: MA

3
Community Action Team
INDUSTRY: Non-Profit
AGENCY: Marc Posch
Design, Inc.
LOCATION: Los Angeles, CA

BRICK BY BRICK

The campaign to rebuild Glen Cedar park

1

2

Your Future Workforce Starts Here

3

1
**The Campaign for
Glen Cedar Park**
INDUSTRY: Non-Profit
AGENCY: Lebow
LOCATION: Toronto, Canada

2
Universitat Bonn
INDUSTRY: Education
AGENCY: Odigy
LOCATION: Brunei Darussalam

3
Aruspex, Inc.
INDUSTRY: Human Resources
AGENCY: Marc Posch
for Spiralgroup
LOCATION: San Francisco, CA

1

2

3

1
Lone Bison Partners, LLC
INDUSTRY: Investment
Consultants
AGENCY: Version-X Design Corp
LOCATION: Burbank, CA

2
The Ark Pet Spa & Hotel
INDUSTRY: Pet Care
AGENCY: Maycreate Idea
Group
LOCATION: Chattanooga, TN

3
Self-Promotion
INDUSTRY: Design
AGENCY: Rizco Design
LOCATION: Manasquan, NJ

Paw Print Publications
INDUSTRY: Book Publisher
AGENCY: TLC Graphics
LOCATION: Austin, TX

inunison
BRANDING

1

™

CITYTECH

2

Lavanderia
Gaudenzi
www.lavanderiagaudenzi.it

3

1
In:Unison Branding
INDUSTRY: Advertising &
Marketing
AGENCY: Handcrafted Media
LOCATION: AL

2
CityTech
INDUSTRY: IT, Networking
AGENCY: Rule29
LOCATION: Geneva, IL

3
Lavanderia Gaudenzi
INDUSTRY: Industrial Laundry
AGENCY: Zerokw
LOCATION: Pesaro, Italy

alpenrose

1

Granite Bay Energy

2

MILL VALLEY
FILM FESTIVAL

3

BOSS

4

1
Rimi Baltic
INDUSTRY: Retail Food
AGENCY: Daymon Worldwide
Design
LOCATION: Stamford, CT

2
Granite Bay Energy
INDUSTRY: Utility
AGENCY: William Salit Design
LOCATION: San Francisco, CA

3
California Film Institute
INDUSTRY: Arts & Entertainment
AGENCY: MINE™
LOCATION: San Francisco, CA

4
BIG BOSS
INDUSTRY: IT Technologies
AGENCY: Graphic Design
Studio by Yurko Gutsulyak
LOCATION: Kyiv, Ukraine

1

2

3

4

1
HBK Investments
INDUSTRY: Investment Banking
AGENCY: Flux Business
Communications
LOCATION: Culver City, CA

2
Pie Town Productions
INDUSTRY: Production Company
AGENCY: YESDESIGNGROUP
LOCATION: Los Angeles, CA

3
Bexley Chamber of Commerce
INDUSTRY: Business
Development
AGENCY: Scott Adams
Design Associates
LOCATION: Minneapolis, MN

4
Self-Promotion
INDUSTRY: Design
AGENCY: Burn Creative
LOCATION: Carlisle, PA

1

2

greenpass

3

1
Codigo Arquitectura
INDUSTRY: Architecture
AGENCY: AxiomaCero
LOCATION: Nuevo Leon, Mexico

2
Svartlamon & Co.
INDUSTRY: Community
AGENCY: UREDD
LOCATION: Trondheim, Norway

3
GreenPass
INDUSTRY: Environmental
AGENCY: Graphicgranola
LOCATION: Austin, TX

Blue Room SalonSpa

INDUSTRY: Spas

AGENCY: Open Creative Group

LOCATION: Birmingham, AL

1

2

1
Out Of The Box
INDUSTRY: Retail Store
AGENCY: Ten26 Design Group, Inc.
LOCATION: Crystal Lake, IL

2
Runaway Dorothy
INDUSTRY: Music Industry
AGENCY: Airtype Studio
LOCATION: Winston-Salem, NC

1

2

3

4

1
Global Health Strategies
INDUSTRY: Health
AGENCY: Empax, Inc.
LOCATION: New York, NY

2
Arteis
INDUSTRY: Internet
AGENCY: GaxDesign
LOCATION: Guadalajara,
Mexico

3
BBC
INDUSTRY: Broadcasting
AGENCY: Empax inc
LOCATION: New York, NY

4
Senterline Communications
INDUSTRY: Social Media
Marketing
AGENCY: Felt Design Group
LOCATION: Costa Mesa, CA

GF&T

1

2

3

1
Global Fire & Technology
INDUSTRY: Construction
AGENCY: Ramp
Creative+Design
LOCATION: Los Angeles, CA

2
Murco
INDUSTRY: Home Demolition
Auctions
AGENCY: SkinnyCorp / Threadless
LOCATION: Chicago, IL

3
Elm Resources
INDUSTRY: Financial
AGENCY: Creative Shoebox, Inc.
LOCATION: CA

1

2

3

1

Artthrob

INDUSTRY: Design

AGENCY: Rebekah Albrecht
Graphic Design

LOCATION: Los Angeles, CA

2

S.C. MIOCOM S.R.L

INDUSTRY: Women Products

AGENCY: Bogdan Terente

LOCATION: Iasi, Romania

3

Village Ridge Boutique

INDUSTRY: Hotel Hospitality

AGENCY: Richard Baird Ltd.

LOCATION: Nottingham, UK

1

2

3

4

1
Yellow Tail
INDUSTRY: Fishing Accessories
AGENCY: Logoholik
LOCATION: Belgrade, Serbia

2
SmartTech
INDUSTRY: Technology
AGENCY: projectGRAPHICS.EU
LOCATION: Prishtina, Kosova,
Albania

3
Grundfaktor
INDUSTRY: Art & Design
AGENCY: Ocular Ink
LOCATION: Nashville, TN

4
**Microfinance Currency
Risk Solutions**
INDUSTRY: Finance
AGENCY: Communication
Via Design
LOCATION: Boston, MA

FoodPhotoBlog.com
INDUSTRY: Food Blog
AGENCY: Siah Design
LOCATION: Milk River, AB,
Canada

Wish Event Productions
NDUSTRY: Event Production
& Catering
AGENCY: Camp Creative Group
LOCATION: Blue Ridge
Summit, PA

1

2

3

1
Mobileciti
INDUSTRY: Cellular / Mobile
Devices
AGENCY: Niedermeier Design
LOCATION: Seattle, WA

2
Tony Flora
INDUSTRY: Real-Estate
AGENCY: Entz Creative
LOCATION: Singapore

3
Milbank Real Estate
INDUSTRY: Construction
AGENCY: Flux Business
Communications
LOCATION: Culver City, CA

1

2

3

1
Pluglife.org
INDUSTRY: Non-Profit
AGENCY: Koren Nelson Design
LOCATION: Los Angeles, CA

2
Master Electricians
INDUSTRY: Electrical
AGENCY: Entz Creative
LOCATION: Singapore

3
Plugged.com
INDUSTRY: Online Dating
AGENCY: D&Dre Creative
LOCATION: Round Rock, TX

1

3

1

New Sheridan Hotel
INDUSTRY: Hospitality
AGENCY: Urban Influence
LOCATION: Seattle, WA

2

Eddie Bauer
INDUSTRY: Apparel & Outdoor Gear
AGENCY: Weather Control
LOCATION: Seattle, WA

1

3

1

Fremont Community School
INDUSTRY: Education
AGENCY: Riverbed
LOCATION: Seattle, WA

2

Four Bridges Food Group
INDUSTRY: Food/Restaurant
AGENCY: Maycreate Idea Group
LOCATION: Chattanooga, TN

1

2

3

1
Changing Qi
INDUSTRY: Non-Profit
AGENCY: YESDESIGNGROUP
LOCATION: Los Angeles, CA

2
Canon Development America
INDUSTRY: Office Products
AGENCY: Ramp Creative+Design
LOCATION: Los Angeles, CA

3
Center for Faith and Enterprise
INDUSTRY: Non-Profit
AGENCY: Marc Posch Design, Inc.
LOCATION: Los Angeles, CA

1

2

3

4

1	2	3	4
Rimi Baltic	**Tides Foundation, USA**	**Juicepop**	**Vitamin Angels**
INDUSTRY: Retail Food	INDUSTRY: Non-Profit	INDUSTRY: Beverage	INDUSTRY: Non-Profit
AGENCY: Daymon Worldwide Design	AGENCY: Kosta Mijie	AGENCY: Mlassiter.com	AGENCY: Breedlove Creative
LOCATION: Stamford, CT	LOCATION: Serbia	LOCATION: Durham, NC	LOCATION: San Diego, CA

1

ZYDOWSKY CONSULTANTS

2

3

charles vincent george
ARCHITECTS

4

1
Glenfinnan Music
INDUSTRY: Music
AGENCY: Rebekah Albrecht
Graphic Design
LOCATION: Los Angeles, CA

2
Zydowsky Consultants
INDUSTRY: Public Relations
AGENCY: Wing Chan
Design, Inc.
LOCATION: New York, NY

3
Documedia Group
INDUSTRY: Entertainment
AGENCY: Rebekah Albrecht
Graphic Design
LOCATION: Los Angeles, CA

4
CVG Architects
INDUSTRY: Architecture
AGENCY: Rule29
LOCATION: Geneva, IL

1

2

3

4

1
Forkwire.com
INDUSTRY: Online Restaurant
Directory
AGENCY: Logoholik
LOCATION: Belgrade, Serbia

2
Stora Enso North America
INDUSTRY: Paper
AGENCY: Gee + Chung Design
LOCATION: San Francisco, CA

3
Bocconi
INDUSTRY: Food / Restaurant
AGENCY: Triad Design Group
LOCATION: Bluffton, SC

4
Events With Taste
INDUSTRY: Food / Restaurant
AGENCY: Maycreate
Idea Group
LOCATION: Chattanooga, TN

1

2

3

4

1	2	3	4
Animal Matters	**Phat Kats**	**SNAUT.com**	**Hello Beads**
INDUSTRY: Education	INDUSTRY: Erotic Toys	INDUSTRY: Design	INDUSTRY: Retail
AGENCY: Felt Design Group	AGENCY: Masood Bukhari	AGENCY: SNAUT.com	AGENCY: Truly Ace
LOCATION: Costa Mesa, CA	LOCATION: Bronx, NY	LOCATION: Los Angeles, CA	LOCATION: Birmingham, UK

1

2

3

4

1	2	3	4
Supergenius Media Services	**Little Leapers Daycare**	**Symbiotic Solutions**	**Volunteers of the Burbank Animal Shelter**
INDUSTRY: DVD Authoring	INDUSTRY: Education	INDUSTRY: Design	INDUSTRY: Non-Profit
AGENCY: Weather Control	AGENCY: D&Dre Creative	AGENCY: Symbiotic Solutions	AGENCY: Rebekah Albrecht Graphic Design
LOCATION: Seattle, WA	LOCATION: Round Rock, TX	LOCATION: Lansing, MI	LOCATION: Los Angeles, CA

Olive and Sinclair
Chocolate Company
INDUSTRY: Food
AGENCY: Anderson Design Group
LOCATION: Nashville, TN

1

THE PLACE TO CIAO!

2

3

4

1

**Nervous Dog Coffee
Bar & Roaster**
INDUSTRY: Coffee /Restaurant
AGENCY: Plug Media Group
LOCATION: Kingwood, TX

2

Schussler Creative
INDUSTRY: Restaurants
AGENCY: Levy Restaurants
LOCATION: Chicago, IL

3

Cable Car Cinema & Cafe
INDUSTRY: Entertainment
AGENCY: Alphabet Arm
LOCATION: Boston, MA

4

Taylor Made Construction
INDUSTRY: Construction
AGENCY: Airtype Studio
LOCATION: Winston-Salem, NC

1

3

2

4

1
Edgeangling.com
INDUSTRY: Outdoor Sports
AGENCY: Roskelly Inc.
LOCATION: Portsmouth, RI

2
Vista
INDUSTRY: Real Estate
AGENCY: Masood Bukhari
LOCATION: Bronx, NY

3
Regan Auto Works
INDUSTRY: Auto Repair
AGENCY: Roskelly Inc.
LOCATION: Portsmouth, RI

4
KornerStop
INDUSTRY: eCommerce
AGENCY: AmericanDesign-Co.com
LOCATION: Los Angeles, CA

CONCEPTORQUE

1

2

EAT **HEALTHY** LIVE **HEALTHY**

3

4

1
ConcepTorque
INDUSTRY: Technology Blog
AGENCY: RDQLUS Creative
LOCATION: Omaha, NE

2
Marco Echevarria
INDUSTRY: Art/Illustration
AGENCY: Burn Creative
LOCATION: Carlisle, PA

3
NRG Bar
INDUSTRY: Food
AGENCY: Alphabet Arm
LOCATION: Boston, MA

4
Buck Hill, Inc.
INDUSTRY: Halloween Attraction
AGENCY: Squarelogo Design
LOCATION: Lakeville, MN

1

2

3

4

1

Kristina Hart
INDUSTRY: Consultant
AGENCY: Storm Corporate
Design
LOCATION: Auckland,
New Zealand

2

Tmiint.com
INDUSTRY: Consultancy
AGENCY: Logoholik
LOCATION: Belgrade, Serbia

3

Visually Sound, ltd.
INDUSTRY: Audio/Video
AGENCY: Nickolas Narczewski
LOCATION: Plano, IL

4

Next for Small Business
INDUSTRY: Consulting
AGENCY: AmericanDesign-
Co.com
LOCATION: Los Angeles, CA

1

2

3

4

1

**Works Progress
Administration**

INDUSTRY: Entertainment

AGENCY: Communication
via Design

LOCATION: Boston, MA

2

Valley Attorney Service

INDUSTRY: Law

AGENCY: Entz Creative

LOCATION: Singapore

3

The Bloom Companies

INDUSTRY: Architecture

AGENCY: Caroline Cruz Design

LOCATION: Silver Spring, MD

4

Lioneye Capital

INDUSTRY: Financial

AGENCY: Remo Strada Design

LOCATION: Lincroft, NJ

1

2

3

4

1
uRefer
INDUSTRY: Online Referral
Marketing
AGENCY: Pryor Design
Company
LOCATION: Ann Arbor, MI

2
Ace
INDUSTRY: Auto Glass
AGENCY: Theory Associates
LOCATION: San Francisco, CA

3
Taste NYC
INDUSTRY: Online Food
Review Service
AGENCY: Sandals Resorts
LOCATION: Miami, FL

4
**Southern Hills
Baptist Church**
INDUSTRY: Religion
AGENCY: Matcha Design
LOCATION: Tulsa, OK

1

PRECISION

2

SCHRANGHAMER
DESIGN GROUP

3

4

1
Matt Worden -
Home on the Range
INDUSTRY: Club Night
AGENCY: David Caunce &
Jan Barker
LOCATION: Manchester, UK

2
Precision Construction
INDUSTRY: Construction
AGENCY: Maycreate
Idea Group
LOCATION: Chattanooga, TN

3
Schranghamer Design Group
INDUSTRY: Interior Design
AGENCY: Alphabet Arm
LOCATION: Boston, MA

4
First & Hope Restaurant
INDUSTRY: Food / Restaurant
AGENCY: Marc Posch
Design, Inc.
LOCATION: Los Angeles, CA

DEBRA'S FURTOGRAPHY

1

Bake & Beans
360° Fresh

2

oxychem

3

1
Debra's Furtography
INDUSTRY: Photography
AGENCY: Senior Creative
Professional
LOCATION: San Francisco,CA

2
Cheetal Foods Limited
INDUSTRY: Bakery & Cafe
AGENCY: Storm Corporate
Design
LOCATION: Auckland,
New Zealand

3
Oxychem
INDUSTRY: Chemical Disposal
& Materials Handling
AGENCY: D&Dre Creative
LOCATION: Round Rock,TX

1

2

1
Trainwreck Saloon
INDUSTRY: Restaurant
AGENCY: Bright Rain Creative
LOCATION: Maryland Heights,
MO

2
Metro Parks Tacoma
INDUSTRY: Outdoor / Nature
AGENCY: Clockwork Studios
LOCATION: San Antonio, TX

1

2

3

4

1	2	3	4
Cap Sur Mer	**Nourish**	**Re:Vive Bodywork**	**Globeat Restaurants**
INDUSTRY: Food	INDUSTRY: Health & Beauty	INDUSTRY: Day Spa	INDUSTRY: Food / Restaurant
AGENCY: Gemini 3D	AGENCY: Clockwork Studios	AGENCY: UNIT Design	AGENCY: Flux Business
LOCATION: Ã_les de la	LOCATION: San Antonio, TX	Collective	Communications
Madeleine, QC, Canada		LOCATION: San Francisco, CA	LOCATION: Culver City, CA

1

2

3

4

1
Marquis Services, Inc.
INDUSTRY: Food Service
Management
AGENCY: Brainchild Collective
LOCATION: Richmond, VA

2
Matizmo Ltd.
INDUSTRY: Design, Marketing
AGENCY: Entz Creative
LOCATION: Singapore

3
Mimi
INDUSTRY: Food
AGENCY: HA Design
LOCATION: Glendora, CA

4
Metrolina Greenhouses
INDUSTRY: Agricultural
AGENCY: The Greater
Good Design
LOCATION: Saint Cloud, FL

1

2

3

4

1

Eddie Bauer
INDUSTRY: Outdoor Apparel
AGENCY: Weather Control
LOCATION: Seattle, WA

2

Milton Taylor
INDUSTRY: Health & Beauty
AGENCY: Moxie Sozo
LOCATION: Boulder, CO

3

Sierra Designs
INDUSTRY: Outdoor Gear
& Apparel
AGENCY: Moxie Sozo
LOCATION: Boulder, CO

4

Fingerprint Communications
INDUSTRY: Public Relations
AGENCY: YESDESIGNGROUP
LOCATION: Los Angeles, CA

1

2

3

1
Freewheel Press
INDUSTRY: Letterpess Printers
AGENCY: CreateTWO
LOCATION: Auburn, AL

2
Eddie Bauer
INDUSTRY: Outdoor Apparel
AGENCY: Weather Control
LOCATION: Seattle, WA

3
Full Circle Cafe
INDUSTRY: Restaurant
AGENCY: Graphicgranola
LOCATION: Austin, TX

1

2

3

4

1
Supermarket
INDUSTRY: Fashion
AGENCY: We Recommend
LOCATION: Copenhagen,
Denmark

2
Radio Language • Germany
INDUSTRY: Broadcasting
AGENCY: Oakley Design
Studios
LOCATION: Portland, OR

3
Refresh Digital
INDUSTRY: Advertising Agency
AGENCY: Con Kennedy
Visual Communications
LOCATION: Dublin, Ireland

4
Summit
INDUSTRY: Food / Restaurant
AGENCY: Mirko Ilic Corp
LOCATION: New York, NY

1

2

3

4

1
Self-Promotion
INDUSTRY: Design
AGENCY: Rizco Design
LOCATION: Manasquan, NJ

2
EarthBar
INDUSTRY: Retail / Health Food
AGENCY: AkarStudios
LOCATION: Santa Monica, CA

4
**Southern Hills
Baptist Church**
INDUSTRY: Religion
AGENCY: Matcha Design
LOCATION: Tulsa, OK

4
Energy Savings Plus
INDUSTRY: Energy Auditing
AGENCY: Enzo Creative
LOCATION: Summit, NJ

REDVIKING

1

MILLER & GREEN

2

ANDREWS LUCIA
WEALTH MANAGEMENT

3

ROOMS
INC

4

1
Red Viking
Insurance Company
INDUSTRY: Insurance
AGENCY: Talbot Design
Group, Inc.
LOCATION: Westlake Village, CA

2
Miller & Green
INDUSTRY: Hair Salon
AGENCY: Landor Associates
LOCATION: Paris, France

3
Andrews Lucia Wealth
Management
INDUSTRY: Finance
AGENCY: Entz Creative
LOCATION: Singapore

4
Rooms Inc.
INDUSTRY: Interior Design
AGENCY: skinnyCorp /
Threadless
LOCATION: Chicago, IL

Reds BBQ
INDUSTRY: Resturant
AGENCY: Masood Bukhari
LOCATION: Bronx, NY

1

2

3

1	2	3
Chihuahua Dance Studio	**The Leasing Studio**	**Fountain Equity Partners**
INDUSTRY: Dance / Arts	INDUSTRY: Leasing & Development	INDUSTRY: Real-Estate
AGENCY: Neil T. McDonald	AGENCY: Urban Influence	AGENCY: Flux Business Communications
LOCATION: Glasgow, Lanarkshire, UK	LOCATION: Seattle, WA	LOCATION: Culver City, CA

WILLOW CREEK

1

WHISKEY CREEK
ORGANICS

2

WINNING WATERS
RANCH

3

1
**Willow Creek Soap
Company**
INDUSTRY: Bath & Body
AGENCY: Carbon Creative
LOCATION: Minneapolis, MN

2
Whiskey Creek Organics
INDUSTRY: Agriculture
AGENCY: Handcrafted Media
LOCATION: Monument, CO

3
Winning Waters Ranch
INDUSTRY: Recreation
AGENCY: Rule29
LOCATION: Geneva, IL

1

2

3

4

1	2	3	4
Accent the Details	**Royal Cheapskate**	**Downtown Properties**	**San Leo Comunal Amministration**
INDUSTRY: Retail	INDUSTRY: Apparel	INDUSTRY: Real-Estate	INDUSTRY: San Leo Tourism
AGENCY: Compass Creative Studio	AGENCY: Ian Lynam Creative Direction & Graphic Design	AGENCY: Flux Business Communications	AGENCY: Zerokw
LOCATION: Burlington, Ontario, Canada	LOCATION: Tokyo, Japan	LOCATION: Culver City, CA	LOCATION: Marche, Pesaro, Italy

1

2

3

4

1	2	3	4
Spin Street Bicycles	**The National Museum of**	**Eddie Bauer**	**Ruby et Violette**
INDUSTRY: retail	**Nuclear Science & History**	INDUSTRY: Apparel &	INDUSTRY: Confections
AGENCY: Simpatico	INDUSTRY: Museum	Outdoor Gear	AGENCY: The O Group
Design Studio	AGENCY: 3 Advertising	AGENCY: Weather Control	LOCATION: New York, NY
LOCATION: Alexandria, VA	LOCATION: Albuquerque, NM	LOCATION: Seattle, WA	

1

2

3

4

1
Webdesign og Foto
INDUSTRY: Web Design /
Photography
AGENCY: Entz Creative
LOCATION: Singapore

2
Santa Monica Eye Group
INDUSTRY: Ophthalmology
AGENCY: AkarStudios
LOCATION: Santa Monica, CA

3
Self-Promotion
INDUSTRY: Design
AGENCY: JohnBoerckel.com
LOCATION: Havertown, PA

4
**Making Invisible
Histories Visible**
INDUSTRY: Education
AGENCY: RDQLUS Creative
LOCATION: Omaha, NE

1

2

3

4

1
Alaska House, New York
INDUSTRY: Non-profit
AGENCY: Design Grace
LOCATION: Jersey City, NJ

2
Cultimer
INDUSTRY: Food
AGENCY: Gemini 3D
LOCATION: Quebec, Canada

3
**Northern Colorado
Outdoors**
INDUSTRY: Outdoor Adventure
AGENCY: D&Dre Creative
LOCATION: Round Rock, TX

4
Paganova
INDUSTRY: Tourism
AGENCY: Odigy
LOCATION: Brunei Darussalam

1

2

Frozen Bucket

3

1
Pixie Toys
INDUSTRY: Retail
AGENCY: Kimberly Schwede
Graphic Design & Illustration
LOCATION: San Francisco, CA

2
Aroha Designs
by Ginnie Hazlett
INDUSTRY: Jewelry
AGENCY: Kimberly Schwede
Graphic Design & Illustration
LOCATION: San Francisco, CA

3
Frozen Bucket
INDUSTRY: Food & Beverage
AGENCY: Kimberly Schwede
Graphic Design & Illustration
LOCATION: San Francisco, CA

MyFashionPlate™.com
INDUSTRY: Online Wardrobe
Consultants
AGENCY: The UXB
LOCATION: Beverly Hills, CA

whitepicket

1

2

gean PUBLISHING

3

1
White Picket
INDUSTRY: Home Improvement
AGENCY: skinnyCorp /
Threadless
LOCATION: Chicago, IL

2
Roots and Wisdom
INDUSTRY: Non-Profit
AGENCY: Aurora Design
LOCATION: Niskayuna, NY

3
Philip Varriale
INDUSTRY: Publishing
AGENCY: Ana Paula Rodrigues
Design
LOCATION: Newark, NJ

1

2

3

1
Austin Walks
INDUSTRY: Health & Fitness
AGENCY: Graphicgranola
LOCATION: Austin, TX

2
Schuylkill Health
INDUSTRY: Healthcare
AGENCY: BrandSavvy, Inc.
LOCATION: Highlands Ranch, CO

3
Wilson Mainee, Inc.
INDUSTRY: Water Delivery
AGENCY: Say Agency
LOCATION: Buenos Aires,
Argentina

1

2

3

4

1

**Southern Hills
Baptist Church**
INDUSTRY: Religion
AGENCY: Matcha Design
LOCATION: Tulsa, OK

2

Park Community Church
INDUSTRY: Religious
AGENCY: Hexanine
LOCATION: Chicago, IL

3

Montimedia
INDUSTRY: IT / Internet ISP
AGENCY: Studio
Threefiftyseven
LOCATION: Adelaide, Australia

4

Autobus Sillons
INDUSTRY: Transport
AGENCY: Gemini 3D
LOCATION: Quebec, Canada

KILOWATT
BIKES

1

Clean Dog
Toelettatura e articoli per animali

2

appdec

3

Tawasul
Electronic Network Solutions

4

1
Kilowatt Electric Bikes
INDUSTRY: Electric Bike
Manufacturer
AGENCY: Creative Squall
LOCATION: Trophy Club, TX

2
Clean Dog
INDUSTRY: Retail
AGENCY: Designaside
LOCATION: Italy

3
Appdec
INDUSTRY: Software
Development
AGENCY: projectGRAPHICS.EU
LOCATION: Prishtina, Kosova,
Albania

4
Tawasul
INDUSTRY: Telecom
AGENCY: Storm Corporate
Design
LOCATION: Auckland,
New Zealand

OPTIMET

1

2

3

4

1
Optimet
INDUSTRY: Ultra Thin Metals
AGENCY: Faulkner Advertising
LOCATION: Santa Barbara, CA

2
Tava
INDUSTRY: Food / Restaurant
AGENCY: AkarStudios
LOCATION: Santa Monica, CA

3
W.A.S. Inc
INDUSTRY: Automotive
AGENCY: DSN
LOCATION: Warsaw, Poland

4
Zyb
INDUSTRY: IT
AGENCY: We Recommend
LOCATION: Copenhagen, Denmark

1

2

1
Nerdcore
INDUSTRY: Marketing
AGENCY: Hexanine
LOCATION: Chicago, IL

2
Self-Promotion
INDUSTRY: Design
AGENCY: The Vega Project
LOCATION: San Francisco, CA

fashionworks

1

début

2

harvest **urban** market   harvest **urban** market   harvest **urban** market

3

1
FashionWorks
INDUSTRY: Non-Profit
AGENCY: Wibye Advertising
& Graphic Design
LOCATION: London, UK

2
Self-Promotion
INDUSTRY: Design
AGENCY: Debut Design Ltd
LOCATION: Wolverhampton, UK

3
Harvest Urban Market
INDUSTRY: Food
AGENCY: William Salit Design
LOCATION: San Francisco, CA

1

2

3

4

1
Paisley Plum
INDUSTRY: Giftware
AGENCY: Triad Design Group
LOCATION: Bluffton, SC

2
Clavin
INDUSTRY: House Service
AGENCY: Mamordesign
LOCATION: Islamic Republic
of Iran

3
Christians in the Visual Arts
INDUSTRY: Non-Profit
AGENCY: Sooy+Co.
LOCATION: Elyria, OH

4
2 Guys Uncorked
INDUSTRY: Wine Blog
AGENCY: Ocular Ink
LOCATION: Nashville, TN

Colonial Beach
BAPTIST CHURCH
A Lighthouse for God

1

Centro Books

2

3

THE
FINAL TOUCH
APPRAISAL SERVICE

4

1
**Colonial Beach
Baptist Church**
INDUSTRY: Religion
AGENCY: Design Nut, LLC
LOCATION: Kensington, MD

2
Centro Books
INDUSTRY: Publisher
AGENCY: Burn Creative
LOCATION: Carlisle, PA

3
Self-Promotion
INDUSTRY: Design
AGENCY: Fernando Rodriguez, Inc.
LOCATION: Santo Domminigo, Dominican Republic

4
**The Final Touch
Appraisal Service**
INDUSTRY: Insurance
AGENCY: UNIT Design Collective
LOCATION: San Francisco, CA

1

2

1
Judson Design Associates
INDUSTRY: Design
AGENCY: Honest Bros.
LOCATION: Denver, CO

2
Penny Chan
INDUSTRY: Food / Restaurant
AGENCY: OJO Design Limited
LOCATION: Sheung Wan,
Hong Kong

1

4

3

2

1

VSona
INDUSTRY: Streaming Video
AGENCY: Geyrhalter Design
LOCATION: Santa Monica, CA

2

Vyn Flowers Inc.
INDUSTRY: Wholesale
AGENCY: Compass Creative
Studio
LOCATION: Burlington, Ontario,
Canada

3

X Form Studio
INDUSTRY: Design
AGENCY: DSN
LOCATION: Warsaw, Poland

4

Intava
INDUSTRY: Retail Technology
AGENCY: Niedermeier Design
LOCATION: Seattle, WA

1

2

3

4

1
**Community Foundation
of Greater Chattanooga**
INDUSTRY: Non-profit
AGENCY: Maycreate Idea Group
LOCATION: Chattanooga, TN

2
**Turku Region
Development Centre**
INDUSTRY: Developer
AGENCY: Zeeland
LOCATION: Turko, Finland

3
Royer's Flowers & Gifts
INDUSTRY: Retail
AGENCY: Go Welsh
LOCATION: Lancaster, PA

4
Wes Wilson
INDUSTRY: Online Store
AGENCY: Ocular Ink
LOCATION: Nashville, TN

LOGO
LICIOUS!

INDEX

288 172, 188
2CREATIVO 153, 156, 244, 259
3 ADVERTISING 65, 70, 168, 313
3RD EDGE COMMUNICATIONS 108, 160, 211

A

AGITPROP DESIGN & COMMUNICATIONS 180
AIRTYPE STUDIO 144, 190, 194, 229, 275, 293
AKARSTUDIOS 91, 105, 160, 182, 208, 223, 307, 314, 322
ALEXANDER EGGER 102, 149, 152
ALEX MIREA CREATIVE STUDIO 111, 120,
ALTEREGO 204, 207, 250
ALLEN CREATIVE 70
ALLISON LENT 56
ALPHABET ARM 127, 137, 159, 214, 224, 226, 232, 257, 293, 295, 299
AMERICANDESIGN-CO.COM 235, 294, 296
ANA PAULA RODRIGUES DESIGN
115, 133, 318
ANDERSON DESIGN GROUP 213, 292
ANDY GABBERT DESIGN 182, 216
ARTVERSION 117
AXIOMACERO 207, 273
AURORA DESIGN 318
AUTOMATIC PARTNERS, LLC 206
AVIVE 255, 256

B

BBMG 125, 161,
BARKER, JAN 299
BECKERS, JOHN 218
BERTZ DESIGN GROUP 56
B.G. DESIGN 262
BIGWIG DESIGN 136
BIZ R 192, 217
BLACKBOOKS 63, 144
BLACKSPOT DESIGNS 40
BLVD DESIGN STUDIO 132
BOGDAN TERENTE 178, 278
BRAINCHILD COLLECTIVE 303
BRANDSAVVY, INC. 222, 245, 260, 319
BREEDLOVE CREATIVE 173, 229, 250, 264, 287

BRIGHT RAIN CREATIVE 43, 301
BRONSON MA CREATIVE 42, 47, 57, 70, 82, 90, 101, 105, 181, 191, 247
BUKHARI, MASOOD 89, 102, 290, 294, 309
BURN CREATIVE 43, 71, 272, 295, 326

C

CALAGRAPHIC DESIGN 193
CAMP CREATIVE GROUP 260, 281
CARACOL CONSULTORES 42
CARBON CREATIVE 311
CAROLINE CRUZ DESIGN 297
CARSTEN, MIKE 223
CAUCE, DAVID 299
CELLAR DOOR CREATIVE 71
CHEMI MONTES DESIGN 229
CLOCKWORK STUDIOS 59, 128, 225, 230, 246, 301, 302
COLORYN STUDIO 224, 234
COMMUNICATION VIA DESIGN 279, 297
COMPASS CREATIVE STUDIO 50, 312, 328
CON KENNEDY VISUAL COMMUNICATIONS 306
CHRIS PIASCIK 121
CHURCH LOGO GALLERY 50
CREATETWO 305
CREATIVE MADHOUSE 42, 70, 74
CREATIVE SHOEBOX, INC. 277
CREATIVE SQUALL 154, 155, 184, 199, 240, 251, 321
CRUMBLED DOG DESIGN 114
CUBIQDESIGN 169, 227, 250

D

D4 CREATIVE GROUP 175, 179, 186, 196, 245
D&DRE CREATIVE 40, 52, 53, 66, 80, 85, 105, 171, 173, 177, 180, 235, 253, 283, 291, 300, 315
DANIEL GREEN EYE-D DESIGN 81
DANIEL ROTHIER 132
DANNY GOLDBERG DESIGN 42, 149
DAVIDPCRAWFORD.COM 75, 117, 225
DAYMON WORLDWIDE DESIGN 115, 271, 287

DEBUT DESIGN LTD. 324
DEFTELING DESIGN 256
DESIGNASIDE 166, 167, 321
DESIGN GRACE 315
DESIGN INTERVENTION 134
DESIGN JUNE 159
DESIGNLAB, INC. 87, 133, 141
DESIGN NUT, LLC 196, 326
DESIGN SOURCE CREATIVE, INC. 67
DEVON 54, 55
DIOGRAFIC 112, 113, 174
DIVERSIFIED APPAREL 94
DOGSTAR DESIGN 49, 57, 80, 95, 238
DONER 125
DOUG BARRETT DESIGN 246
DSN 322, 328

E

ELLIOT 72, 139,
EMPAX, INC. 276
ENTZ CREATIVE 128, 139, 155, 163, 172, 178, 179, 183, 241, 255, 256, 258, 282, 283, 303, 308, 314
ENZO CREATIVE 116, 307
EYE-D DESIGN 81

F

FAULKNER ADVERTISING 322
FELT DESIGN GROUP 51, 174, 276, 290
FERNANDO RODRIGUEZ, INC. 238, 326
FIFTH LETTER 60, 67, 237
FIVE VISUAL COMMUNICATION & DESIGN 194
FLUX BUSINESS COMMUNICATIONS 248, 272, 282, 302, 310, 312
FOAN82 147, 155, 159
FOX FIRE CREATIVE 213
FRANK & PROPER 170
FRANK D'ASTOLFO DESIGN 103
FRAN ROSA SOLER 72, 243

G

GAXDESIGN 209, 220, 237, 256, 276
GEE + CHUNG DESIGN 44, 45, 60, 64, 230, 289
GEMINI 3D 302, 315, 320

GEYRHALTER DESIGN   158, 161, 180, 181, 187, 328
GO WELSH   329
GRACE FELLOWSHIP CHURCH   61, 62, 92
GRAPHIC DESIGN STUDIO BY YURKO GUTSULYAK   77, 86, 242, 271
GRAPHICGRANOLA   273, 305, 319
GRAPHIC IMPACT   177
GREATER GOOD DESIGN, THE   62, 303

H

HA DESIGN   303
HAMES DESIGN   90, 174
HANDCRAFTED MEDIA   198, 270, 311
HEXANINE   84, 111, 143, 320, 323
HL2   210
HOLY COW CREATIVE   246
HONEST BROS.   121, 135, 327
HOPSCOTCH STUDIO   172
HORNALL ANDERSON   76, 163,
HOUSEMOUSE   130, 185, 215, 230
HOUSE OF TEARS DESIGN   201

I

IAN LYNAM CREATIVE DIRECTION & GRAPHIC DESIGN   84, 104, 118, 120, 131, 139, 146, 153, 159, 166, 180, 192, 212, 218, 241, 243, 312
IDAPOSTLE   46, 95
IMAGEBOX PRODUCTIONS, INC.141, 231, 254
IMAGINE   167, 172, 236
INSANEFACILITIES   126

J

JACK TOM DESIGN   59, 63, 78
JAMES MARSH DESIGN   171
JOHN BECKERS   218
JOHNBOERCKEL.COM   227, 314
JUST CREATIVE DESIGN   168

K

KAIMERE   243
KALICO DESIGN   121, 212
KENNETH DISENO   51, 78, 201, 227
KIMBERLY SCHWEDE GRAPHIC DESIGN &

ILLUSTRATION   316
KO11 DESIGN   154, 190
KOLANO DESIGN   165, 184
KOMPREHENSIVE DESIGN   226
KOREN NELSON DESIGN   260, 265, 283
KOSTA MIJIC   261, 287
KROG   68, 103, 104, 162, 165, 247

L

LANDOR ASSOCIATES   177, 308
LANGTON CHERUBINO GROUP   148, 251
LAUGHING LION DESIGN   196
LEBOW   66, 267
LEGACY DESIGN GROUP   197
LESCHINSKI DESIGN   48, 162
LEVY RESTAURANTS   61, 144, 200, 206, 293
LITTLE JACKET   92, 127, 248
LITTLE UTOPIA, INC.   158
LOGOHOLIK   55, 79, 84, 96, 100, 149, 279, 289, 296
LOGOMANIC   134, 145
LSDSPACE   48, 63, 64, 78, 87, 93, 99, 100, 101, 112, 122

M

MABU   113, 122
MAMORDESIGN   143, 325
MARC POSCH DESIGN, INC. 151, 249, 264, 266, 267, 286, 299
MARIANA PABON   104, 157, 205, 220
MARQUIS DESIGN   184
MARY HUTCHISON DESIGN, LLC   58, 167,
MASOOD BUKHARI   89, 102, 290, 294, 309
MATCHA DESIGN   142, 187, 227, 298, 307, 320
MATLI GROUP   173
MAYCREATE IDEA GROUP   96, 142, 151, 162, 182, 212, 265, 268, 285, 289, 299, 329
MAZZIOTTI DESIGN   168, 263
MBCREATIVE   92, 137,
MCBREEN DESIGN, INC.   51, 86
MCMILLIAN DESIGN   50

MEDIAWORKS   226
MFDI   94
MILLER CREATIVE, LLC   208
MILLER MEIERS DESIGN FOR COMMUNICATION   126
MINE   50, 64, 65, 73, 77, 86, 87, 111, 122, 133, 151, 171, 271
MIRKO ILIC CORP.   65, 67, 95, 96, 102, 114, 158, 165, 306
MLASSITER.COM   287
MOHOGRAPHIC INC.   266
MOXIE SOZO   68, 176, 178, 217, 240, 260, 304

N

NALINDESIGN   118, 239
NEXTBIGTHING   123, 162,
NICKOLAS NARCZEWSKI   100, 115, 296
NICO AMMANN   216
NIEL T. MCDONALD   75, 90, 120, 310
NIEDERMEIER DESIGN   61, 64, 65, 71, 81, 82, 86, 97, 103, 143, 215, 244, 247, 258, 282, 328
NILS-PETTER EDWALK   146
NP GRAPHIC DESIGN   83, 181

O

OAKLEY DESIGN STUDIOS   58, 71, 75, 77, 123, 131, 175, 186, 228, 262, 306
OCULAR INK   132, 161, 254, 258, 279, 325, 329
ODIGY   58, 138, 147, 201, 239, 240, 267, 315
O GROUP, THE   189, 313
OHTWENTYONE   60, 241
OJO DESIGN LIMITED   327
OPEN CREATIVE GROUP 220, 221, 255, 274
ORANGE BIKE DESIGN   46, 129, 140, 251

P

PAPER TOWER   154, 207
PARALELOZ   175
PARALLEL PRACTICE, LLC.   142
PARLIAMENT   131
PAUL SNOWDEN   81

Periscope 209, 233
Plazm 135, 228
Plug Media Group 293
Pratt Institute 208
projectGRAPHICS.EU 101, 116, 140, 158, 209, 216, 251, 279, 321
Pryor Design Company 160, 189, 191, 249, 298

Q

Q 47, 73, 80, 116, 117, 139, 143, 163, 166,

R

Ramp Creative +Design 72, 81, 103, 246, 264, 277, 286
Razor Creative 60
RDQLUS Creative 263, 295, 314
Reactor, LLC 78, 126
Rebecca Carroll 121
Rebekah Albrecht Graphic Design 73, 278, 288, 291
Reebok International 170, 177
Remo Strada Design 91, 253, 297
Ribbons of Red 209
Richard Baird Ltd. 166, 278
Riley Designs 66, 183
Rizco Design 163, 167, 250, 268, 307
ripe.com 51, 76, 77, 265
Riverbed 112, 140, 285
Roskelly Inc. 41, 48, 54, 62, 69, 87, 91, 93, 97, 134, 234, 245, 253, 294
Roycroft Design 152
Rubin Design 206
Rule29 168, 235, 238, 261, 270, 288, 311

S

Sabrah Maple Design 265
Sage Systems 266
Saltmine, The 131, 219
Sandals Resorts 245, 298
SandorMax 247
Say Agency 186, 319
Scott Adams Design Associates 68, 152, 272
Scott Creative 204
Scott Ott Design 43, 99
Senior Creative Professional 300
Siah Design 110, 230, 231, 280
Silver Creative Group 154
Simpatico Design Studio 313
skinnyCorp 149, 277, 308, 318
SNAUT.com 208, 290
Solak Design Co. 43, 89
Sonet Digital 152
Sooy+Co. 325
Snowden, Paul 81
Spiralgroup 267
Splash:Design 170
Squarelogo Design 76, 88, 295
Stefan Romanu 72, 76, 93, 98, 138, 216
Stellar Debris 48, 248
Stressdesign 116, 197
Storm Corporate Design 93, 115, 122, 140, 178, 224, 296, 300, 321
Studio ThreeFiftySeven 254, 320
Studio GT&P 55, 155
Subcommunication 75, 120, 136, 249
Symbiotic Solutions 228, 291
Synthview 212

T

Talbot Design Group, Inc. 148, 259, 308
Tangent Graphic 104, 141, 195
Ten26 Design Group, Inc. 123, 134, 190, 275
Threadless 149, 277, 308, 318
Theory Associates 41, 298
The Greater Good Design 259, 263
The O Group 189, 313
The Saltmine 131, 219
The UXB 119, 195, 197, 317
The Vega Project 117, 323
Thinkhaus 127, 189, 199, 258
Tinged 79
TLC Graphics 269
Tracey Ortolano 133
Tread Creative 146
Triad Design Group 289, 325
Truly Ace 290
TwolineSTUDIO 187
Tyler Sticka 248

U

Unexpected Ways 41
UNIT Design Collective 108, 111, 114, 150, 160, 181, 193, 201, 219, 223, 302, 326
Urban Influence 94, 114, 284, 310
UREDD 130, 147, 174, 273

V

VanPelt Creative 217
Vega Project, The 117, 323
Version-X Design Corp. 221, 268

W

Weather Control 46, 59, 108, 109, 125, 127, 130, 136, 137, 164, 198, 205, 213, 229, 284, 291, 304, 305, 313
We Recommend 123, 124, 146, 150, 151, 165, 184, 189, 190, 306, 322
Whatislight 213
Wholesome Design 252
Wibye Advertising & Graphic Design 226, 324
William Salit Design 254, 271, 324
Wing Chan Design, Inc. 255, 288

X

XYARTS 54, 55, 79, 88, 91, 204, 253

Y

YESDESIGNGROUP 183, 272, 286, 304
YIU Studio 150, 161, 234, 261
Yurko Gutsulyak 77, 86, 242, 271
YYES 175, 228, 238

Z

Z2 Marketing + Design 234
Zeeland 329
zerokw 194, 231, 240, 241, 270, 312

SPECIAL THANKS

To Nancy Heinonen, for her vision and support.

To Shachar Lavi, who managed the design production
and never missed a beat.

To the brilliant panel of judges, who helped pick this
excellent collection.

And to all the talented designers, who submitted
their delicious work.

Love to you,

Peleg